PHILIP ROTH

MODERN LITERATURE SERIES

GENERAL EDITOR: Philip Winsor

In the same series:

S. Y. AGNON   *Harold Fisch*
SHERWOOD ANDERSON   *Welford Dunaway Taylor*
LEONID ANDREYEV   *Josephine M. Newcombe*
ISAAC BABEL   *R. W. Hallett*
JAMES BALDWIN   *Carolyn Wedin Sylvander*
SIMONE DE BEAUVOIR   *Robert Cottrell*
SAUL BELLOW   *Brigitte Scheer-Schäzler*
BERTOLT BRECHT   *Willy Haas*
JORGE LUIS BORGES   *George R. McMurray*
ALBERT CAMUS   *Carol Petersen*
TRUMAN CAPOTE   *Helen S. Garson*
WILLA CATHER   *Dorothy Tuck McFarland*
JOHN CHEEVER   *Samuel T. Coale*
COLETTE   *Robert Cottrell*
JOSEPH CONRAD   *Martin Tucker*
JULIO CORTÁZAR   *Evelyn Picon Garfield*
JOAN DIDION   *Katherine Usher Henderson*
JOHN DOS PASSOS   *George J. Becker*
THEODORE DREISER   *James Lundquist*
FRIEDRICH DÜRRENMATT   *Armin Arnold*
T. S. ELIOT   *Joachim Seyppel*
WILLIAM FAULKNER   *Joachim Seyppel*
F. SCOTT FITZGERALD   *Rose Adrienne Gallo*
FORD MADOX FORD   *Sondra J. Stang*
JOHN FOWLES   *Barry N. Olshen*
MAX FRISCH   *Carol Petersen*
ROBERT FROST   *Elaine Barry*
GABRIEL GARCÍA MÁRQUEZ   *George R. McMurray*
MAKSIM GORKI   *Gerhard Habermann*
GÜNTER GRASS   *Kurt Lothar Tank*
ROBERT GRAVES   *Katherine Snipes*
PETER HANDKE   *Nicholas Hern*
LILLIAN HELLMAN   *Doris V. Falk*
ERNEST HEMINGWAY   *Samuel Shaw*
HERMANN HESSE   *Franz Baumer*
CHESTER HIMES   *James Lundquist*
HUGO VON HOFMANNSTHAL   *Lowell W. Bangerter*
CHRISTOPHER ISHERWOOD   *Claude J. Summers*
SARAH ORNE JEWETT   *Josephine Donovan*
UWE JOHNSON   *Mark Boulby*
JAMES JOYCE   *Armin Arnold*
FRANZ KAFKA   *Franz Baumer*
RING LARDNER   *Elizabeth Evans*
D. H. LAWRENCE   *George J. Becker*

(continued on last page)

PHILIP ROTH

Judith Paterson Jones
Guinevera A. Nance

FREDERICK UNGAR PUBLISHING CO.
NEW YORK

Copyright © 1981 by Frederick Ungar Publishing Co., Inc.
Printed in the United States of America
Design by Anita Duncan

Library of Congress Cataloging in Publication Data

Jones, Judith P.
  Philip Roth.

  (Modern literature series)
  Bibliography: p.
  Includes index.
  1. Roth, Philip—Criticism and interpretation.
I. Nance, Guinevera A. II. Title. III. Series:
Modern literature monographs.
PS3568.O55Z73   813'.54   80-53701
ISBN 0-8044-2438-1   AACR2
ISBN 0-8044-6320-4 (pbk.)

Quotations are from Roth's novels and from a collection of his essays, *Reading Myself and Others* (1975).

The authors wish to thank Auburn University at Montgomery for sabbatical leaves during which portions of this book were written. Guinevera Nance is especially grateful to Philip Roth for an interview on April 9, 1979, in London and for his continued encouragement. Judith Jones wishes to thank the National Endowment for the Humanities and Professor Ralph Freedman of Princeton University for a fellowship which facilitated research on this book.

Contents

Chronology

1933   Born March 19 in Newark, New Jersey, to Herman and Bess Finkel Roth.

1946–50   Attends Weequahic High School, Newark.

1950–51   Attends Newark College, Rutgers University.

1951–54   Attends Bucknell University. Receives B.A. in English, *magna cum laude*; Phi Beta Kappa.

1955   Receives M.A. in English from University of Chicago. Enlists in army; discharged due to back injury.

1956–57   Ph.D. candidate and Instructor of English, University of Chicago. "The Contest for Aaron Gold" published in *Epoch,* selected for one of *The Best American Short Stories of 1956.*

1959   February 22, marries Margaret Martinson Williams. Publishes *Goodbye, Columbus.* Receives the Jewish Book Council's Daroff Award for *Goodbye, Columbus; Paris Review*'s Aga Khan Award for "Epstein"; "The Conversion of the Jews" collected in *The Best American Short Stories of 1959.*

1960   Receives National Book Award for *Goodbye, Columbus.* "Defender of the Faith" collected in *The Best American Short Stories of 1960* and *The O. Henry Prize Stories* of 1960. Joins the faculty of the Iowa Writers Workshop.

1962   Publishes *Letting Go.* Writer-in-residence, Princeton University. Ford Foundation grant in playwriting.

1963   Is legally separated from Margaret Martinson Roth.

1964   "Novotny's Pain" selected for *The O. Henry Prize Stories* of 1964.

1965   Begins teaching at the University of Pennsylvania.

1967   Publishes *When She Was Good*.

1968   Margaret Martinson Roth dies in an automobile accident.

1969   Publishes *Portnoy's Complaint*. Paramount film of *Goodbye, Columbus*.

1970   Is elected to the National Institute of Arts and Letters.

1971   Publishes *Our Gang. Unlikely Heroes* (a dramatic adaptation of three short stories) opens in New York.

1972   Publishes *The Breast*. Warner Brothers film of *Portnoy's Complaint*.

1973   Publishes *The Great American Novel*.

1974   Publishes *My Life as a Man*.

1975   Publishes *Reading Myself and Others*. Becomes general editor of the "Writers from the Other Europe" series for Penguin Books.

1977   Publishes *The Professor of Desire*.

1979   Publishes *The Ghost Writer*.

1980   Publishes *A Philip Roth Reader*.

1981   Publishes *Zuckerman Unbound*.

Introduction:
Written and Unwritten Worlds

Sensitive to his public reputation and reticent about his personal history, Philip Roth has managed to keep the man who is billed on one of his book covers as "America's most controversial novelist" largely hidden from biographers. When Roth talks about himself in print, as he does to any extent only in *Reading Myself and Others,* he takes an almost academic stance toward himself and his work. In this collection of essays and interviews, he discloses Roth the man only in relationship to Roth the writer and, concerned with the governing aesthetic principles of the fiction, "reads" his work somewhat as a literary theorist might. Even in surveying his essays and responses to interviewers, Roth finds a controlling idea among his various perspectives; he points out in the introduction to *Reading Myself and Others* that the twenty-three pieces in the book reveal his preoccupation with the "relationship between the written and the unwritten world." Roth indicates that this way of distinguishing between the world a writer creates in his fiction and the world of "actuality" in which he lives is more useful to him than the usual dichotomies such as "art and life" or "imagination and reality." It more aptly describes, he suggests, the "worlds that I feel myself shuttling between every day."

Most of what Roth has made accessible to the

1

public about his unwritten world centers on his life in the Jewish milieu of Newark, New Jersey—ironically, because he translated it into the written world of his fiction. In some of his early work and in *Portnoy's Complaint,* the novel that made Roth a millionaire, he relies heavily upon the ethos of the lower-middle-class Jewish neighborhood in the Weequahic section of Newark where he grew up. However, in commenting upon his early attempts to "transform into fiction something of the small world in which I had spent the first eighteen years of my life," Roth indicates that he drew more from the ambience of place than from his personal history or that of his family. Thus, while some of Roth's fiction has the tonal and descriptive authenticity of autobiography, it is not intended to document the life of the man who created it.

Philip Milton Roth, who made the American Jewish family legendary in *Portnoy's Complaint,* is the grandson of native Jewish-Americans on the maternal side and Central European Jewish immigrants on the paternal side. He was born March 19, 1933, in Newark to Herman and Bess Finkel Roth. Apparently, he was the kind of "good" Jewish boy that he burlesques in *Portnoy*—"flowering," as he says, in elementary school, studious and civic-minded at Weequahic High School, where he was a member of the student council and assistant editor of the school newspaper, and respectful at home. Recalling his relationship with his parents during his adolescence, Roth says that he did little to "upset whatever balance of power had enabled our family to come as far as it had and to work as well as it did."

After graduation from high school in 1950, Roth attended the Newark extension of Rutgers University, a point of fact he shares with the young protagonist, Neil Klugman, in *Goodbye, Columbus.* After a year, Roth transferred to Bucknell University. There, in

what he describes as a "respectable Christian atmosphere hardly less constraining than my own particular Jewish upbringing," his intellectual curiosity was
renewed after the long drought of high school. He
edited the literary magazine, was active in drama,
for which he apparently had quite a flair, and was
initiated into Phi Beta Kappa.

Upon graduation from Bucknell with a B.A. in
English in 1954, Roth entered graduate school at the
University of Chicago, where he completed an M.A.
in English in 1955. After serving for a brief time in
the army, he returned to the University of Chicago
as an instructor in English and Ph.D. candidate. It is
the Roth of this period, graduate student and aspiring
writer, that Theodore Solotaroff remembers in "The
Journey of Philip Roth," a piece that has the flavor of
a personal memoir. Solotaroff recalls first meeting Roth
in a course on Henry James, where his literary acumen
and good grooming distinguished him from the other
graduate students. As they became friends, he discovered that they were much alike in temperament—
"aggressive, aloof, moody, and, as graduate students
go, worldly." Roth was writing consistently at this
time, and his work was beginning to be published in
magazines such as *Esquire* and *The New Yorker*. He
left the doctoral program but remained at the University of Chicago for a year as an instructor in the college.
From Solotaroff's perspective at the time, the affluent
young bachelor, who was making his way in the world
as a teacher and a writer, seemed "to have the world
by the tail." [1]

The success of *Goodbye, Columbus,* published
shortly thereafter, in 1959, would seem to indicate
that the twenty-six-year-old Roth did, indeed, have
the world by the tail. His first novella won the National Book Award in 1960 and received the Daroff
Award from the Jewish Book Council of America. It

was also in 1959 that Roth married Margaret Martinson Williams, and in the next year he joined the faculty of the Iowa Writers Workshop as a visiting lecturer.

During the time he was at Iowa on a Guggenheim grant, Roth wrote his first novel, *Letting Go.* Like *Goodbye, Columbus,* it drew upon the ethos of an environment and situation that Roth knew firsthand—in this instance the atmosphere surrounding his days as a graduate student and instructor at the University of Chicago. In 1962 Roth left Iowa to become writer-in-residence at Princeton University, and during 1962–64 he was also visiting writer at the State University of New York at Stony Brook. In 1963, he was legally separated from Margaret Martinson Roth, who died five years later in an automobile accident. Roth's visit in 1972 to Prague, Czechoslovakia, and Kafka's graveside was instrumental in promoting his interest in the writers of Communist Europe and led to his becoming general editor of the "Writers from the Other Europe" series for Penguin Books in 1975.

Almost ten years after *Goodbye, Columbus* launched Roth's writing career with acclaim, he published *Portnoy's Complaint,* a novel in the guise of a confession that caused considerable speculation about the man who wrote it. Roth suddenly found himself famous, he says, "from one end of the continent to the other" and the object of a good deal of "media myth-making." He was the subject of discussion on the "Tonight" show; he was reported to be enjoying a romance with the actress Barbra Streisand in one newspaper column and to have suffered a breakdown in another. In the furor of notoriety, Roth, who says he lacks the temperament for a public life, retreated from his New York apartment and took up residence for a while at the Yaddo Writers' Colony in Saratoga Springs. Now, over ten years after *Portnoy,* Roth, whom one reviewer called a "jet-propelled dervish who whirls through literature, demolishing forms, spinning off royalty checks, and leaving everybody . . . to wonder where he will strike next," lives the relatively quiet life of a writer and part-time teacher.[2]

Although intended to describe his mental traveling between the worlds of fact and fiction, Roth's depiction of himself as "shuttling" between two worlds characterizes his physical traveling as well. For about half the year, he lives in Connecticut, spending some of that time at the University of Pennsylvania, where he teaches. He suggests that almost the whole of his public life takes place in the classroom, where he is allowed to be a literature teacher "instead of Famous." Roth "shuttles" across the Atlantic to spend the rest of the year in London, where he occupies two flats and moves daily between life and work—or, from his perspective, between the written and the unwritten world.

It was in London, in the spring of 1979, that one of the authors met Philip Roth for lunch and a conversation about his work.[3] We had agreed to meet at a small restaurant in Kensington, within walking distance of Roth's writing studio, where he was working on the galleys of *The Ghost Writer*. Obviously an habitué of the place, Roth spoke briefly with a couple at another table before coming to the table that had been reserved for our meeting. Lean, of medium build, and dressed in a black turtleneck, he looked as much the teacher as the world-famous writer. His gracious and soft-spoken manner seemed slightly at odds with the intense figure he generally presents in photographs on book covers and in magazine articles, where he gazes directly and seriously into the camera. Having recently returned from a brief excursion to Morocco, Roth had already settled into a well-established working routine that forbade his having anything more substantial for lunch than paté and

Perrier. He dismissed the idea of taping the interview and settled into the friendly, jocular manner that adds humor to his writing.

Our conversation ranged over his work, his career, and the critical reactions to his fiction. As *Reading Myself and Others* indicates, and as Roth revealed in our discussion, he is a writer who has thought long and deeply about the process of fiction writing and about the fiction he has produced. He seems capable of taking a distanced perspective on his work, moving from statements about authorial intention to the impact of the piece as a whole with the ease of a man who has integrated the fictionist and the scholar. This integrated point of view emerged as we discussed whether sensitive gentile readers would be more fair to his work than many Jewish readers had been. Roth suggested that a gentile reader might have a different "range of tolerance" for his work and made the comparison between the way he would be likely to read Flannery O'Connor [4] and the way a Southerner might. He and the reader more familiar with southern dialect might, he speculated, both be in the same range of interpretation, but there would be a certain patina to O'Connor's work that he would miss. He would also, we surmised, be more tolerant of certain aspects of O'Connor's fiction of which the southern or Catholic reader might be critical. It is this ability to see himself as both writer and reader of fiction that lends balance to the view Roth takes of his own work.

Surveying his career, Roth emphasized a point that undoubtedly has preoccupied him—that his career would have a very different shape and meaning if *Portnoy* were taken out of it. He also indicated that he has done a good deal of work to "put *Portnoy* behind" him and reiterated the comment he had made in *Reading Myself and Others* that *The*

Great American Novel provided him with a means of "getting over" *Portnoy*.

One of the most astonishing aspects of Roth's perspective is his familiarity with the various stances that critics and reviewers have taken on his work. He obviously has his favorites among the pieces that have been written on him and his fiction, and he is able to cite bibliographic references without hesitation. He also has well-articulated theories about why various critics have been antagonistic to his work. Responding to some observations about the view that some feminist criticism has taken on his fiction, Roth admitted that he was perplexed by complaints that his work was antifeminist. He indicated that the critique of men has been evident in his fiction from the beginning and that his intention has been to show the frailty and vulnerability of men rather than to demonstrate causes for male chauvinism. He would be interested, he suggested, in seeing good feminist criticism of his work that recognized his intention of showing male characters as "clay with aspirations."

After a two-hour dialogue with Philip Roth, one comes away with the impression that literature is for him a matter of moral significance and that writing is a means of pleasure. The difference, Roth says, between what he experiences and what he writes is words, and his ability to articulate experience is evident in his conversation as well as his books. Our conversation ended as we walked up the street together and he exited from the main thoroughfare to encounter once again the written world he had created in *The Ghost Writer*.

1

○○

Good Girls and Boys
Gone Bad

In an interview that Roth conducted with himself after the publication of *The Great American Novel,* he indicates that the deliberate "recklessness" of this work proceeded from his having first dealt responsibly and seriously with the subject of restraint. Surveying his previous fiction, Roth recognizes that his attempt generally has been to dramatize the "problematical nature of moral authority and of social restraint and regulation." Since that interview in 1973, it has become obvious that much of Roth's work not only before but also after *The Great American Novel* is concerned with the "question of who or what shall have influence and jurisdiction over one's life."

In broad perspective, the evolution of Roth's fiction over the last twenty years deals with this issue of the individual versus authority and presents an interesting parallel to what might be seen as the natural process of maturation. For example, the child's attempt to deal with the coercive force of the parents constitutes one of the major conflicts in such early works as *Goodbye, Columbus, Letting Go, When She Was Good,* and *Portnoy's Complaint.* In each book, the apparently unresolvable conflict between the desire to love and communicate and the desire to be free of constraint pits children against parents in a deadlocked battle filled with guilt and recrimination. This conflict emerges most clearly in *When She Was Good* and *Portnoy's Complaint,* two very different novels that are, nevertheless, connected by their focus on what Roth has called "a grown child's fury against long-standing authorities believed . . . to have misused their power."

This primary adolescent struggle for self-determination predicts the dramatization of the "grown-up" male-female battle for control that is central in *My Life as a Man* and also foreshadows the theme of the libidinous man's internal conflict over passion and self-restraint as it develops in *The Professor of Desire.* In *My Life as a Man* and *The Professor of Desire,* the issue of freedom and restraint that had previously been fought primarily on the battleground of the family is transferred to several arenas: to marriage and other sexual relationships, to the warring dualities of the self, and to aesthetics, where the artist-professor recognizes in art an expression of the archetypal tension between convention and creativity, between self-control and license.

But this movement from adolescent rebellion to marital strife, to the eternal battle with the self, and then to the concern with the relationship of art to life paints only in the broadest strokes the evolution of the theme of dominion in Roth's fiction. As early as 1959, in the short story "Eli, the Fanatic," Roth dramatized the individual in conflict with forces both outside and inside himself; and, as late as 1979, in *The Ghost Writer,* Roth is still concerned with the son's estrangement from his family and his need both to declare his freedom from his parents and to exonerate himself before them. In his attempts to resist parental authority, however, the protagonist of this brief fiction is clearly not a transmogrified Alexander Portnoy or Lucy Nelson. Compared to their rage, his is a quiet resistance, ameliorated somewhat by his mature efforts both to come to terms with art and to accept the insolubility of family conflict. Thus, while the progression of Roth's fiction has by no means been steadily away from the depiction of the family as the major force to be resisted in the quest for autonomy, over the years his novels have moved generally toward either submerging that issue or integrating it with other, equally important conflicts.

The struggle for personal freedom and identity—for what Roth calls "authority over one's life"—assumes many guises in Roth's fiction, and, consequently, the antagonists are various. Roth describes three of his major characters—Gabe Wallach in *Letting Go*, Alexander Portnoy in *Portnoy's Complaint,* and David Kepesh in *The Breast*—as "three stages of a single explosive projectile that is fired into the barrier that forms one boundary of the individual's identity and experience." It surely is not reductive to visualize several of Roth's protagonists in this way—as projectiles fired both against the limits imposed by their own identities and against imperatives imposed from without.

This dual necessity of coming to terms with the self in the process of resisting what others perceive one to be is central in Roth's fiction. Each time a character resists definition by what is external to him, he is forced to deal with his own sense of himself. Consequently, resistance to the control of the family or the society and their delineation of the boundaries for the individual always involves self-examination on the part of the individual. In many ways, Ozzie Freedman, in the short story "The Conversion of the Jews," speaks for Roth's defiant characters when, after having labeled his rabbi a bastard, he asks himself, "Is it me? Is it me ME ME ME ME!" Accustomed to having been the "good" son, the "good" father, the "good" assimilated Jew, characters such as Ozzie

Freedman, Alex Portnoy, Gabe Wallach, David Kepesh, Nathan Zuckerman, Lou Epstein, and Eli Peck
must engage in much critical self-examination when-
ever they act in a way uncharacteristic of social or
familial expectations and thus contrary to their own
sense of themselves. Personal sovereignty is not
merely a matter of throwing off another's authority; it
also necessitates for these protagonists that they deal,
however ambiguously, with the new "ME" that
emerges out of their refusal to be bound any longer to
another's conception of what is good. That uncharac-
teristically defiant self, labeled now by the family or
the culture as "bad," is, ironically, still fettered by the
indoctrinated self—Portnoy, for example, unmanned
by guilt, Lucy Nelson unhinged by vengeance—but all
the protagonists in Roth's fiction at least make some
attempt to stake a claim for the individualized self
against all the pressures that are at work to restrain it.

Goodbye, Columbus

Of Roth's major characters, Neil Klugman in *Goodbye,
Columbus* most passively accepts the sway of casual
circumstance in his life. In this, Roth's first departure
from the short story, the surface plot is the familiar
theme of the summer romance. Neil Klugman, the
poor Jewish boy from Newark, has a summer affair
with Brenda Patimkin, the affluent Jewish girl from
suburban Short Hills, who is home on vacation from
Radcliffe. Neil spends his vacation from his job at the
library in Newark with Brenda and the Patimkin family, but the love affair dissipates after she returns to
college.

The sense of temporariness and impermanence
that characterizes not only the relationship between
Brenda and Neil but also Neil's whole approach to

life is accentuated by the summer-romance theme and the vacation atmosphere. Admitting that he is "not a planner," Neil drifts through his love affair and his job with the same lack of commitment to permanency. Life for him seems to be a kind of interlude in which nothing in the present has the cast of the future. He constantly reiterates that he does not visualize his job at the library as being forever, and although he considers the possibility of marriage to Brenda as a way to mitigate the transience of their relationship, he lacks the courage to make such a proposal.

Two important and somewhat parallel scenes in the novel illustrate the kind of "Prufrockian" [1] timidity Neil exhibits before the two spheres of love and work in his life. In the first of these, Neil is considering the possibility that after his summer vacation he may be put in charge of the reference room. He is not particularly attracted to the stifling atmosphere of the library; yet in what he describes as his "muscleless devotion" to his work, he finds himself will-lessly "edging towards" the promotion, which he views as entrapment. It is as if he had no choice in the matter—because it is about to happen, it *must* happen. Visualizing this imprisonment over which he seems not to be able to exert his will, Neil considers that "life from now on would be not a throwing off, as it was for Aunt Gladys, and not a gathering in, as it was for Brenda, but a bouncing off—a numbness." At the age of twenty-three, Neil reacts to circumstance like a person etherized.

In the second scene that places in perspective Neil's passivity, his incapacity for commitment made through choice, he contemplates the prospect of asking Brenda to marry him. Living in the Patimkin house for a while, under the shadow of the preparations for Brenda's brother's wedding, reminds him that "separation need not be a permanent state." Curiously enough, but understandable in terms of his fuzzy view

of commitment, Neil thinks of marriage as implying
uncertainty and impermanence rather than security
and union. As if it were a new realization to him,
he suddenly thinks:

People could marry each other, even if they were young!
. . . Well, I loved her, and she me, and things didn't seem
all right at all. Or was I inventing troubles again? I supposed I should really have thought my lot improved con-
siderably; yet, there on the lawn, the August sky seemed
too beautiful and temporary to bear, and I wanted Brenda
to marry me. Marriage, though, was not what I proposed
to her when she drove the car up the driveway, alone,
some fifteen minutes later. That proposal would have taken
a kind of courage that I did not think I had.

Neil's thoughts on the subject of marriage are full of
"yets" and "thoughs," and what he proposes instead
of marriage is that Brenda buy a diaphragm.

In a love affair characterized largely by competition, sterility, and secretiveness, the issue of the diaphragm becomes highly symbolic. It is apparent that,
in part, Neil asks Brenda to buy it in order to test her
willingness to acquiesce to his demands. He wants her
to "just do it. Do it because I asked you to." More important, the buying of the diaphragm comes to represent for Neil a kind of surrogate ritual performed in
the absence of the religious ritual of marriage.

For Neil it is the doctor who weds Brenda to
him, not the rabbi. Void of any spiritual dimension in
his life and critical of the rituals in which others engage, Neil typifies that element in American culture
which opts for a semblance of commitment rather
than the thing itself. He is disengaged, spiritually and
emotionally, and substitutes the profane for the sacra-
mental. In a highly ironic scene that stands out as the
thematic climax, Neil's spiritual vacuousness, attraction to the materialistic and acquisitive life of the

Patimkins, and passive relinquishment of responsibility for his own actions emerge clearly. Waiting for Brenda to be fitted for the diaphragm, Neil wanders into St. Patrick's and begins to "make a little speech" to himself, which he calls a prayer:

God, I said, I am twenty-three years old. I want to make the best of things. Now the doctor is about to wed Brenda to me, and I am not entirely certain this is all for the best. What is it I love, Lord? Why have I chosen? Who is Brenda? The race is to the swift. Should I have stopped to think?

I was getting no answers, but I went on. If we meet You at all, God, it's that we're carnal, and acquisitive, and thereby partake of You. I am carnal, and I know You approve, I just know it. But how carnal can I get? I am acquisitive. Where do I turn now in my acquisitiveness? Where do we meet? Which prize is You?

This "little speech" under the guise of prayer shows that Roth has an ear attuned to the voices of banality and hypocrisy; when he allows a character's damnation to issue from that person's own mouth, he is at his satirical best. Neil's speech is full of clichés such as "All for the best" and "The race is to the swift" intermixed with quotations from the Bible and good old American optimism. It is also filled with emphasis on all-American materialism, the god that seems most important in the novel. In a logic that is contrived to justify his lack of true religious principle, Neil equates encountering God with some kind of ultimate expression of the appetites—both for sex and for "things." This connection between love ("carnality") and materialism ("acquisitiveness") pervades the novel. Although Neil is often critical of the acquisitiveness of the Patimkin family, he is closer to them than he would like to believe. He is not far different from Brenda's uncle, Leo, a pathetic sort of Willy Loman [2] character, who tells a story about one of the two best things that ever happened to him, in which money and sex are linked closely. He is also not radically different from Brenda's parents, who, instead of merely connecting sex and money, make the provision of "things" the measure of parental love. For example, in a letter full of recriminations for Brenda's having betrayed the family by having sex with Neil, Brenda's mother reminds her: "But you drifted away from your family, even though we sent you to the best schools and gave you the best money could buy."

What does finally set Neil apart from the Patimkins in this scene is his inability to accept his own ingenious equation of materialism with the "prize" that is God. Ashamed of his clever but certainly profane prayer, he hears the answer to his question, "Which prize is You?" in the noise of Fifth Avenue: "Which prize do you think, *schmuck?* Gold dinnerware, sporting-goods trees, nectarines, garbage disposals, bumpless noses, Patimkin Sink, Bonwit Teller—"

Once again, Neil is in a kind of limbo that characterizes his condition throughout the novel. If he is reminiscent of Eliot's Prufrock in his timidity before commitment to love and work, he also recalls that character in not being truly at home in either of the two worlds he inhabits—Newark or Short Hills. Attracted to, but repulsed by, the overt acquisitiveness of the Patimkin family, with its "sporting-goods trees" and refrigerators bulging with fruit, he finally cannot commit himself fully to that world of the American Dream of success come true. Yet, at the same time, he is uncomfortable with the world represented in Newark by his Aunt Gladys, where life is a process of "throwing off." Only three choices ever seem very apparent to Neil: throwing off, taking in, and bouncing off.

The disengagement that "throwing off" implies

largely becomes Neil's way of encountering experience. He exemplifies what Stanley Trachtenberg sees
in modern fiction as "the hero in stasis." These recent
heroes, Trachtenberg suggests, are "reluctant either to
confirm their own values or to accept those of society." [3] We might, in fact, go one step further than
Trachtenberg and say of Neil Klugman that not only
is he reluctant to confirm personal or societal values,
he seems to shy away from forging any values what-
soever. In his temporary migration from New Jersey
and his own family to the suburbs and the Patimkin
family, Neil wonders if he might not "learn to become
a Patimkin with ease." Yet, finally, he finds the
competitiveness of the newly upper-middle-class Patimkins as offensive as the humble acceptance of his
own family. All he can manage is skepticism and an
ironic view of each of these sets of values, but he can
find nothing with which to replace them.

Neil's one unambivalent relationship is with a
young black boy who comes to the library to look at
pictures of Gauguin's paintings. Like Neil, the child is
a fugitive from home, and his euphoric "that's the
fuckin life" when he sees Gauguin's representations of
Tahiti mirrors Neil's astonishment when he drives into
the suburbs and realizes that it seemed "as though
the hundred and eighty feet that the suburbs rose in
altitude above Newark brought one closer to heaven."
That he and the boy are somehow linked becomes
clear to Neil when he dreams that they are on a ship
anchored at an island paradise. Against their will,
however, the ship begins to move out of the harbor,
and the natives bid them farewell with "Goodbye,
Columbus . . . goodbye, Columbus . . . goodbye. . . ."
It is important to realize that Roth makes this dream
seem improbably probable by connecting the "Goodbye, Columbus" to the sound of the record Neil had
heard coming from Brenda's brother's room before he

fell asleep. The record Ron plays is a nostalgic remi-
niscence about the homecoming game at Ohio State
University in 1956 and other such memorable occa-
sions, culminating in a melodramatic farewell to the
university: "We offer ourselves to you then, world,
and come to you in search of Life. . . . We will miss
you, in the fall, in the winter, in the spring, but some
day we shall return. Till then, goodbye, Ohio State,
goodbye, red and white, goodbye, Columbus . . .
goodbye, Columbus . . . goodbye. . . ."

Out of these two sequences, of course, Roth
draws the title for his novel. Both episodes revolve
around a reluctant leave-taking and a voyage into
the unknown. In Neil's dream, he is a reluctant version of the explorer Columbus, and his destination is
unknown to him. In Ron's record, he and the other
seniors at Ohio State are to venture out from Columbus, Ohio, into the world, in search of "Life." The implications are that neither Neil nor Ron has before
him a clear sense of where the voyage will culminate,
but certainly for Ron there is a clearer sense of moorings to which he can return. Ron is being forced to let
go of something he has actually had; Neil is cut adrift
from something he knows only in a dream. Finally,
Neil becomes an ironic representation of the explorer
who prefers to stay within the safety of a fantasy
paradise rather than chart his own mysterious future.

Through the dream sequence Neil's unconscious
reflects a mode of existence that is also evident in his
life. Both dreaming and waking, he is unable to will
himself to any action other than drifting with the
tide of circumstance. In the dream he sees himself
and the little black boy on the boat, and "the boat
was moving and there was nothing he could do about
it." The image recalls his seemingly powerless "edging towards" what he envisions as a life of numbness
in the library. It also characterizes the drift of his rela-

tionship with Brenda. Partially "wooed and won on Patimkin fruit"—on the abundance of possessions in the Patimkin way of life—Neil still seems incapable of any permanent attachment to Brenda. After her mother finds the diaphragm and it is clear that Brenda faces the crucial choice between loyalty to her parents, who equate love with material provisions, and devotion to Neil, who offers her little more than occasional sex under the name of love, the affair simply dissipates.

Neil leaves the hotel and walks to Harvard Yard, where he stands before the Lamont Library and becomes as introspective as he is ever shown to be in the novel. He looks at the image of himself in the library window, but that external image offers him no clue about what is inside him. Finally, he wonders: "What was it inside me that had turned pursuit and clutching into love, and then turned it inside out again? What was it that had turned winning into losing, and losing—who knows—into winning? I was sure I had loved Brenda, though standing there, I knew I couldn't any longer." As in his dream, the boat is moving, and Neil thinks there is nothing he can do about it. One moment he thought he loved Brenda, and now he is sure that it is no longer possible. Ironically, he does not even know whether in losing Brenda he has won or lost. He uses here the same kind of language of competition he had used earlier in his little speech to God, when he had affirmed that the "race is to the swift" and had questioned "which prize" was God.

But if this is a vocabulary that Neil has acquired during his brief exchange with the Patimkin family, it is apparent that he does not use it with the same force or conviction as that family does. He lacks the energy that Ron, the athlete, has for competition, and he lacks the gusto with which Mr. Patimkin attempts to beat out the competition in his quest for the everlasting dollar. The irony is that while Neil's inability to force himself into the Patimkin mold is certainly to his credit, he is unable to come up with any viable alternative to the values that the Patimkins represent.

Only in the last two sentences of the novel does Roth suggest the prospect that Neil may be beginning a journey away from aimless noninvolvement and toward commitment to something he has chosen; and, even there, the cryptic nature of the passage leaves its significance open to interpretation. As the sun rises on the first day of the Jewish New Year, Neil arrives back in Newark in "plenty of time for work." If, for a moment, Neil recognizes an image of his disordered life as he looks through the windows of the library and sees a "broken wall of books, imperfectly shelved," the deliberateness with which he returns to Newark and his work may mark the beginning of an attempt to arrange his life in a more meaningful pattern. John N. McDaniel suggests that at the end of the book Neil is Roth's version of the activist hero who is "still in the process of 'becoming' a fully-realized self." [4] While there is little evidence of any activism on Neil's part, the ending does suggest that the reluctant "Columbus" of this book may be on the brink of becoming a somewhat more deliberate voyager.

Although it deals principally with the passivity with which its protagonist faces the risks of commitment, in tracing Neil Klugman's exodus from Newark to Short Hills and his return to Newark, *Goodbye, Columbus* introduces several other themes, most of which recur in Roth's fiction. Among these are the difficulties of love and communication, the confusion between generous and acquisitive instincts, the duality inherent in the necessity and yet impossibility of the family, and the tendencies toward moral and spiritual degeneration of modern American life, with the latter two ideas carrying the fullest weight of Roth's satire. Yet, ironically, the satire is realized largely through Neil's perspective. Lacking in much else, Neil is, nevertheless, clear-sighted enough to recognize in the manipulations of his and Brenda's families and in the shallowness of the Patimkin affluence values that he cannot, ultimately, accept as his own. This is one of the few Roth novels in which the protagonist's parents are not a significant presence; and perhaps, in part, because Neil's parents are removed from the action of the novel by having been dispatched to the neutral territory of Arizona, Mr. and Mrs. Patimkin take center stage as the "prototypic" parents. That there is some connection between Neil's family and the Patimkin family, however, despite their differences in social status, becomes apparent when Neil meets the Patimkins at the dinner table:

Mr. Patimkin reminded me of my father. . . . He was tall, strong, ungrammatical, and a ferocious eater. When he attacked his salad—after drenching it in bottled French dressing—the veins swelled under the heavy skin of his forearm.

Described by Neil as "Brobdingnags" [5] because of their mealtime gusto, the Patimkins are associated throughout the novel with a bounteous plenty of food and with consumption that substitutes for communication. As the observer in the novel, Neil comments:

There was not much dinner conversation; eating was heavy and methodical and serious, and it would be just as well to record all that was said in one swoop, rather than indicate the sentences lost in the passing of food, the words gurgled into mouthfuls, the syntax chopped and forgotten in heapings, spillings, and gorgings.

The Patimkins are the exemplars of the American Dream come true. They have a table, a refrigerator, a house stuffed with material goods; they have a storeroom full of old furniture to serve as a reminder of their roots in Newark. In the language of American idealism, they have "made it"; yet despite the Patimkins' poshly educated children, nose jobs, and suburban country-club life, the relationships within the family are not particularly satisfying. Brenda fights with her mother and manipulates her father to get what she wants. She tells Neil that her father is "not too smart but he's sweet at least." For her mother, Brenda forgoes even that much kindness. She responds to her parents in terms of the goods they provide for her, and they, in turn, equate their goodness toward her with material possessions.

Hurt at the discovery that Brenda has been having an affair with Neil, both Mr. and Mrs. Patimkin write to her, and their letters show the extent to which each characteristically relates to her in terms of money. Mr. Patimkin, always protective of Brenda against her mother, urges: "Don't pay any Attention to your Mother's Letter when you get it. I love you honey if you want a coat I'll buy You a coat." There is no pause, no punctuation, between "I love you" and "I'll buy you a coat." It is as if, in the father's mind, love and buying were synonymous. Mrs. Patimkin's letter also reveals the link between love and what money provides, and makes the connection in a way that implies manipulation. Reminding Brenda that they sent her to the best schools and gave her "the best money could buy," Mrs. Patimkin concludes her letter with, "You have broken your parents' hearts and you should know that. This is some thank you for all we gave you."

The implications here are that love is a kind of commercial deal: the parents gave the daughter "things" (a measure of love), and in exchange she owes them a certain kind of behavior. Mrs. Patimkin feels betrayed because Brenda has not lived up to her end of the bargain—she has not returned the "right" behavior for what she has received. After a final argument with Neil over whether her obligation is to him or her parents, Brenda reveals the extent to which she has been bought and to which she has accepted the materialistic, impersonal, nonspiritual value system of her family: "They're still my parents. They did send me to the best schools, didn't they? They have given me everything I've wanted, haven't they?" In the end, Brenda too opts for the Patimkin version of the Great American Dream of love and money.

In defending himself against a charge of being "grimly deterministic," Roth maintains that the "business of *choosing* is the primary occupation of any number of my characters. I am thinking of souls even so mildly troubled as Neil Klugman and Brenda Patimkin, the protagonists of the novella *Goodbye, Columbus.*" In *Goodbye, Columbus* the most obvious set of values to be chosen or rejected are those which the Patimkins represent. Brenda chooses the prize that comes with being the good little Patimkin daughter. Neil ultimately rejects that prize, not so much because he has consciously chosen to do so but because Brenda's rejection of him in favor of her parents makes that choice no longer accessible to him. Both attracted to and repulsed by the Patimkin acquisitiveness, Neil exists in a limbo of indecisiveness until he is forced to "look hard at the image" of himself. He then begins his journey back to Newark, which has positive implications for his finally beginning to make some order of his life.

Goodbye, Columbus: The Short Stories

Goodbye, Columbus contains not only the title piece but also five of Roth's short stories. Among these,

"Epstein," "The Conversion of the Jews," and "Eli, the
Fanatic" are thematically consonant with the novella
in their concern with the conflicts associated with
love, the family, and the difficulties of communication
in a world in which materialism has replaced spiri-
tuality. These stories also introduce another theme
that will pervade Roth's later books and which exists,
submerged, in *Goodbye, Columbus*. This theme ema-
nates from Roth's representation of the individual in a
society that values "normality" and conformity more
than the development of the individual. In the essay in which he maintains that choosing is the "primary occupation" of protagonists like Neil Klugman
and Brenda Patimkin, Roth goes on to make choosing the principal activity of the characters in his short
stories as well. He says:

Then there are the central characters in the stories published along with *Goodbye, Columbus*, "Defender of the
Faith," "The Conversion of the Jews," "Epstein," "Eli, the
Fanatic," and "You Can't Tell a Man by the Song He
Sings," each of whom is seen making a conscious, deliberate, even willful choice *beyond* the boundary lines of
his life, and just so as to give expression to what in his
spirit will not be grimly determined, by others, or even
by what he had himself taken to be his own nature.

All the major characters in these short stories, in the
process of resisting the dominion of others over their
lives, must also resist their own previous acceptance
of the roles that the family, society, and the people
they love have said they should play. As always, the
struggle for the Roth protagonist is complicated by
the duality of an enemy that is at the same time internal and external.

   Of the three stories, "Epstein" connects most
closely to the dual themes of family restraint and the
conflict of the individual identity with the social ex-

pectations he and those around him have imbibed. A stalwart father and successful first-generation American businessman, Lou Epstein feels at fifty-nine that "everything is being taken away from him." His son Herbie, who was to have been heir to the Epstein Paper Bag Company, is dead of polio; his rosy-complexioned baby Sheila has grown into a pimply, fat socialist who curses him for being a capitalist; and his once beautiful and sexually adventurous wife, Goldie, has become an unappetizing cooking and cleaning machine with pendulous breasts, who smells like Bab-O.

One night, Epstein's discovery of his nephew passionately making love on the living room floor with the girl from across the street, Linda Kaufman, finally jolts him into realizing the full extent of his impoverishment and leads him to an emotional and sexual involvement with Ida Kaufman, Linda's widowed mother. The result is comedy that borders on the tragic. Epstein develops a rash that he fears indicates syphilis; and in a comic scene in which everyone in the house winds up in Epstein's and Goldie's bedroom, Goldie declares that she wants a divorce. Displaced from his bedroom and from his usual duties as husband and father, Epstein seeks refuge in Ida Kaufman's house, where he has a heart attack. In the final scene, Goldie asserts her prerogative as Lou's wife and rides beside him in the ambulance, urging him to come to his senses and live a normal life.

Like many of the fathers in Roth's fiction, Epstein has accepted fully the responsibilities of citizenship, marriage, and parenthood but has missed out on pleasure. He has lived a sensible, structured life of conformity to the images his culture has taught him. Pleading his case to his nephew, Michael, after he has been banished from his own bedroom, Epstein offers the rationale that has governed his life: "All my life I tried. I swear it, I should drop dead on the spot, if all my life I didn't try to do right, to give my family what I didn't have. . . ." The irony of this statement is fully realized in the double meaning of Epstein's attempting to give what he "didn't have." The surface meaning is, of course, that Epstein has tried to provide for his family those material possessions which he had not had. But the submerged implication is that Epstein tried to give his family what he did not have to give. He has tried to give them a self duty-bound to accept the loss of his dreams—to be a "good" father and a "good" husband despite the little he receives in return. The affair with Ida, however, causes him to confront an uncharacteristic side of himself—a side that is passionate and, more significant, adulterous. As Roth points out in one of his essays, Epstein's adultery does not "square with the man's own conception of himself." Having acted in a way contrary to what he had perceived to be his own nature, Epstein sounds like so many of Roth's characters when they exceed the limits of the image that they and others have of them: "I don't even feel any more like Lou Epstein."

If Lou sees his actions as uncharacteristic, his wife regards them as positively aberrant. Ordered, meticulous, and resolute, Goldie is associated repeatedly in the story with cleanliness, restriction, and normality. When she is told by the doctor in the ambulance that Lou can recover if he will forgo trying to act like a boy and live a life normal for sixty, Goldie repeats his message as if it were an incantation: "You hear the doctor, Lou. All you got to do is live a normal life." Much of the pathos of this story turns on the meaning of the normal life. Experiencing it as attrition and restriction, Lou has, for a time, attempted to free himself; but, as Roth says in synopsizing the story, "in the end, Epstein . . . is caught—caught by his family, and caught and struck down by exhaustion, decay, and disappointment, against all of which he had set out to make a final struggle." The extent to which Epstein is caught is evident in the last lines of the story. The doctor assures Goldie that he can cure Epstein's rash "so it'll never come back," and Epstein's grim future is forecast in his words.

"Epstein" is one of Roth's short stories that has attracted considerable hostility from the Jewish community. It has drawn charges of anti-Semitism against Roth and has been condemned for presenting a negative picture of Jews in America. In defending himself and the story against readers who resent the presentation of an adulterous Jew, Roth reasonably asserts that his interest is principally in the man Epstein, not the Jew, and that his focus on a man who is an adulterer is intended primarily to reveal the condition of the man. That the adulterous man is a Jew seems, in itself, to set up the kind of internal conflict Roth wishes to explore in a character who "acts counter to what he considers to be his 'best self,' or what others assume it to be, or would like it to be." Part of Epstein's sense of his "best self" is inextricably tied up with the religious and cultural fact of his being Jewish, with all the attitudes toward marriage, the family, and adultery that socialization implies; and it is with his acting contrary to that image of himself that Roth the fictionist becomes engaged.

This emphasis upon fidelity to "characterological" truth rather than moralistic truth leads Roth to make some important distinctions between the apologist and the artist and between moralism and literature. He maintains that it is not the purpose of fiction to "affirm the principles and beliefs that everybody seems to hold" but rather to free our feelings from societal restrictions so that we may respond to imaginative experience without the compulsion to judge in the same way that we would in everyday experience, where we might be expected to act on our judgments. "Ceasing for a while to be upright citizens," Roth suggests, "we drop into another layer of consciousness. And this expansion of moral consciousness, this exploration of moral fantasy, is of considerable value to man and to society."

In "The Conversion of the Jews," written when Roth was twenty-three, moral fantasy and moral fable are intertwined. As in "Epstein," Roth explores the dilemma of the individual caught by his family and in conflict with the constraints of his immediate environment, but this story is less realistically rooted than "Epstein." Elsewhere, Roth calls it a "daydream" and describes it in a way that suggests its fabulous qualities: "A good boy named Freedman brings to his knees a bad rabbi named Binder (and various other overlords) and then takes wing from the synagogue into the vastness of space." On a less mythical level, the story deals with religious myopia, cultural limitation, and power. Ozzie Freedman, a young student in the Hebrew school of Rabbi Binder, comes into conflict with his teacher when the rabbi contends that Jesus was historical but not divine and that a virgin birth defies biological possibility. Building on the logic that God was omnipotent in making what he wished, when he wished, during the six days of the Creation, Ozzie reasons that surely God could "let a woman have a baby without having intercourse."

Binder's insistence on a major difference between Judaism and Christianity—that Christ was human but not God—and Ozzie's refusal to deny that God could make anything he chose leads to a physical confrontation in the classroom. For the second time, Ozzie is struck in the face over the issue of God's omnipotence and Christ's divinity. When his mother had learned why he was once again in trouble with the "authorities," she had hit Ozzie across the face "for the first time in their life together." When Rabbi Binder strikes Ozzie, the boy flees to the roof of the building, after calling his teacher a bastard. Amazed at the extent of his defiance, Ozzie Freedman on the roof of the synagogue confronts an unrealized side of his nature and, at the same time, comes to discover the meaning of power. Because the crowd below, which eventually includes the rabbi, his fellow students, his mother, and the fire department, construes Ozzie's taking refuge on the roof as a threat that he will jump, Ozzie turns their fears against them and begins to control the crowd by threatening to jump. Seeing Rabbi Binder on his knees in an unprecedented pose of supplication, Ozzie realizes the full extent of his power and makes everyone kneel in "the Gentile posture of prayer." He begins to catechize the rabbi and then his mother, making them both admit that God can "make a child without intercourse," and, finally, he extracts from everyone in the crowd a verbalization that they believe in Jesus Christ.

Having accomplished at least a ritualistic, if not actual, conversion of the Jews, Ozzie directs his final demand to his mother—a promise that she will never "hit anybody about God." The religious symbolism that pervades the story and the positiveness with which Roth obviously intends to present Ozzie Freedman are accentuated in the concluding line, when Ozzie jumps "right into the center of the yellow net that glowed in the evening's edge like an overgrown halo."

On the level at which "The Conversion of the Jews" reads like a fable, with Ozzie *Freed*man's personifying the urge for individualistic freedom and Rabbi *Bind*er the social and religious constrictions which seek to bind that freedom, the story suggests that defiance is heroic when one's soul is in jeopardy.

It also illustrates in a general way, through its focus on the particular constraints imposed by the Jewish community, that the sustaining influences of family and culture are also often the most powerful forces working to inhibit the spiritual and psychological development of the individual. The soul-battered Ozzie is literally driven to defiance out of frustration when he is forced either to deny his own perceptions and be "good" or to deny the teachings of religion and family and be "bad." Such a double bind leaves him with no clear-cut options.

Bernard F. Rodgers, Jr., has suggested that a parallel exists between Ozzie's position and that of the young Roth during and after the writing of *Goodbye, Columbus*. He sees "The Conversion of the Jews" functioning as

an effective metaphor for the pressures of the Jewish community which combine with the self-righteousness of its young author to prompt the satiric thrust of *Goodbye, Columbus* itself. Rabbi Binder, Mrs. Freedman, and Yakov Blotnik personify all that Roth was determined to reject in the attitudes of the Jewish environment which had surrounded him for the first eighteen years of his life; and Ozzie Freedman's adolescent revolt against their xenophobia and closed-mindedness, their constant concern for "what-is-good-for-the-Jews," reflects Roth's own artistic revolt.[6]

Although in approaching the story metaphorically Rodgers makes some questionable assumptions about Roth's intention—that he was "determined" to reject portions of his early Jewish environment, for example—he appropriately suggests that the piece is grounded in personal experience. Roth's comments on the story indicate that he wrote from what he knew. He says that it "reveals at its most innocent stage of development a budding concern with the oppressiveness of family feeling and with the binding ideas of religious exclusiveness which I had experienced first-hand in ordinary American-Jewish life." Out of this early personal knowledge of constraint, Roth has proceeded to construct a diversity of fictional worlds in which the characters attempt to work through a dispute over control between themselves and some outside authority; thus "The Conversion of the Jews" occupies an important place in Roth's career—as the first indication of a concern that becomes pervasive.

"Eli, the Fanatic" bridges the predominant themes of "Epstein" and "The Conversion of the Jews" on the one hand and *Goodbye, Columbus* on the other. It recalls "Epstein" in its presentation of an uncertain and somewhat pathetic man in conflict with what he and others around him regard as normal, and it extends the "what-is-good-for-the-Jews" attitude of "The Conversion of the Jews" in a way that becomes ironic in light of the previous story. It also anticipates Roth's emphasis in *Goodbye, Columbus* on the moral and spiritual vacuousness of the assimilated, suburban Jew whose pursuit of the materialistic American Dream has cut him off from the sustaining aspects of Jewish culture and tradition.

Eli Peck, the "fanatic" in this story whose title ironically takes the perspective of those opposed to him, is a successful Jewish lawyer living in the secular suburb of Woodenton (Wooden Town). He and his Jewish friends have been assimilated into the once exclusively gentile community by distinguishing themselves as little as possible from the Gentiles—by seeking to become largely inconspicuous as Jews. They manage successfully to secure a peaceful coexistence out of this compromise until a group of Orthodox Jews—displaced persons from Germany—establish a "yeshivah"[7] in the community and disturb the security of the assimilated Jews by being in dress and manner conspicuously Jewish. Particularly offended

by one of the emissaries from the school who comes
into town dressed in an antiquated black suit and
a talmudic hat, whom they refer to as the "greenie,"
the Americanized Jews hire Eli Peck to use the law in
ridding them of these reminders of their own difference from the rest of the community—of their Jewishness. Eli's commission as the spokesman for this
Jewish constituency brings him into contact with Leo
Tzuref, the director of the yeshivah, and the mysterious greenie; and from that point the story focuses
predominantly on Eli Peck's strange involvement
with the yeshivah and his progressive identification
with the greenie until, finally, he is dressed in the
greenie's rabbinical garb and becomes his "Doppelgänger," or double. At the conclusion of the story, Eli,
considered insane by his friends and family, has taken
on the characteristics of religious fanaticism that had
previously been associated only with the dispossessed
Orthodox Jews living on the edge of Woodenton.

The story begins with Eli in conflict with Jewish
orthodoxy and ends with him in conflict with modern,
assimilated Jewishness. Initially, in speaking for the
progressive upper-middle-class Jews of Woodenton,
Eli urges Leo Tzuref and his companions to conform
to the customs of the community, pointing out that
the amity which Jews and Gentiles have established
has necessitated that each relinquish "some of their
more extreme practices in order not to threaten or offend the other." Ironically, he builds his case for conformity to these remnants of Hitlerian Germany on
the notion that if Jews in prewar Europe had been
less obviously Jewish—had not given offense to those
in power by differentiating themselves from the
"norm"—the persecution of the Jews might not have
occurred. On the continuum from the "normal" to the
"abnormal," the progressive Jews of Woodenton obviously stand in relation to the Orthodox Jews as the

Gentiles in restrictive communities have generally stood in relation to assimilated Jews. The Gentiles have required of the Jews that they conform to traditional, normal American practices in order to live peacefully in the community, and these Americanized Jews, in their turn, require of the yeshivah members that they conform to the standards of their segment of the society in order to live satisfactorily with the Jewish community.

Seen from this perspective, the "what-is-good-for-the-Jews" motif of "The Conversion of the Jews" takes on ironic overtones in this story. In both instances, that which is good for the Jews is whatever protects the Jew from the disapproval of the "goyim" [8]—usually inconspicuousness. In "The Conversion of the Jews," Yakov Blotnik is concerned with Ozzie Freedman's making a spectacle of himself on the roof of the synagogue, and in "Eli, the Fanatic," the assimilated Jews are concerned with the traditional Jews' making a spectacle of their religious distinctiveness.

There are significant differences, however, in the way the two stories deal with what may be called "Jewishness." In "The Conversion of the Jews," Ozzie's intellectual progressiveness is at odds with religious exclusiveness, and Roth treats his resistance to the restrictions of Jewish dogma sympathetically. His unwillingness to conform to what others want him to believe, although perhaps not good for the Jews, is represented as being good for him. In "Eli, the Fanatic," Eli's progressive acculturation is initially at odds with religious orthodoxy, and Roth treats his and the Jewish community's antipathy for Jewish exclusiveness, or distinctiveness, unsympathetically. His and his neighbors' insistence that the refugees from the yeshivah conform to their secular way of life, although perhaps good for the Jews, is represented as being insupportably restrictive and ultimately not good for

the very sensitive Eli. In his own way, the unstable
Eli Peck is as much an identity in flux, seeking to
ground itself in an individuality of its own choosing,
as the adolescent Ozzie Freedman; and when his
compromised modern Jewishness comes up against
uncompromising traditional Jewishness, he seems to
lose his balance.

Whether Eli actually loses his balance or gains it
at last depends entirely upon the perspective one
chooses; and Roth has constructed the story deftly so
that it supports either conclusion. What the Jewish
community and Eli's family regard as insanity, Eli
experiences as revelation. And because the story is
clearly about identity and the standards that define it
as normal or abnormal, the question of how Eli Peck
is finally to be regarded is ironically consistent with
the principal issue of the story. To call him insane
because his behavior is inconsistent with social expectations, or to call him whole because he embraces
a severed portion of his past and comes to know who
he is, implies something about the perspective of the
judge. At the beginning of the story, speaking for
legalism and compromise in his initial encounter with
Leo Tzuref, Eli is clearly associated with the Americanized Jewish community, which desires to rid itself
of an obtrusive reminder of its nonmaterialistic, non-
American, immoderate past. Asked by Tzuref to distinguish his position from that of the community, Eli
responds, "I am them, they are me, Mr. Tzuref." He
is, then, by the standards of his neighbors, sane—normal. But what Eli comes slowly to realize is that he
must say of his relationship to the yeshivah the same
as he has said of his relationship to the Jewish-American community: "I am them, they are me." As he begins to acknowledge his kinship with the "fanatical"
Jews, his neighbors determine that he is insane.

Both the literal and the symbolic indications of

Eli's identification with the Orthodox Jews and with Jewish orthodoxy revolve around clothes. Clothing, in fact, is a central metaphor in the two predominant conflicts in the story—the Jewish community's conflict with the yeshivah and Eli's internal conflict between secular and religious Jewishness. The relation of clothing and identity emerges when Tzuref responds to Eli's insistence that the greenie wear modern attire by saying, "The suit the gentleman wears is all he's got." It becomes clear that Tzuref is referring to the rabbi's identity, his connection with his past, and not to his clothes. The clothes are all that he has of what he was. Later, the connection between appearance and identity reaches its culmination when Eli and the greenie exchange clothing. Putting on the discarded clothing that the greenie has left on his doorstep, Eli feels himself transformed into a Jew. When his suburban neighbor, busy with the meaningful task of painting the rocks in her yard pink, tells him that there is a Jew at his door, Eli responds, "That's me." And when he goes up the hill to the yeshivah dressed in the greenie's garb and encounters the greenie clothed in his own best green suit, Eli at first has the notion that he is two people and then that "he was one person wearing two suits." To Eli, the intermingling of the two identities is so complete that for a moment "his hands went out to button down the collar of his shirt that somebody else was wearing." The "Doppelgänger" motif here indicates that in facing the "fanatic," the rabbinist who stands for the unassimilated Jewish tradition, Eli also confronts a part of himself—that part of his identity represented in his religious and cultural heritage.

When the rabbi, without uttering a word, points down the hill to the town of Woodenton, Eli has a revelation. It is the awareness toward which he has been moving throughout the story—the recognition that he is connected with the Jews of the yeshivah in a way that his fellow American Jews deny. His earlier words, "I am them, they are me," now refer to Old-World Jews rather than modern Jews. Like Moses descending from the mountain with a holy commission, Eli walks down the hill into Woodenton and among those who were his people. For the first time Eli seems to know who he is and to feel that he has the ability to choose. He worries for a moment that he has chosen to be crazy but then decides that it is when a person fails to choose that he is actually crazy. Therefore, he makes a conscious decision to remain in his rabbinical garb as he goes to the hospital to see his newborn son, whose birth happens to coincide with Eli's spiritual rebirth.

The story ends with the hospital attendants humoring Eli long enough to tear off his jacket and give him a sedating shot that "calmed his soul, but did not touch it down where the blackness had reached." Since Eli has associated blackness with the clothes of the rabbi, and Roth has constructed the story so that clothing stands symbolically for identity, the conclusion implies that the spiritual assimilation Eli has achieved remains untouched by sedation. In the sense that normality in this story means moderation, compromise, and alienation from the religious and cultural past, Eli will never be normal again.

In this story, as in "Epstein" and "The Conversion of the Jews," Roth explores the conflicts between conformity and identity, between the individual and his social environment, and the conflict within the individual as he makes a choice that challenges not only what others would like him to be but also his own sense of his "best self." In the introduction of these themes, the stories in the *Goodbye, Columbus* volume are auguries of the predominant issues to emerge in Roth's novels. Throughout his fiction, Roth is preoccu-

pied with the moral imperatives that a person imposes on himself and their relationship to the dictates
of family, culture, and religion. In the absence of
heroes of epic proportion, he draws protagonists characteristically modern in the sense that their battleground is the self and their struggles are with the
forces that shape, and attempt to impose limitations
upon, that identity.

Letting Go

In 1962, three years after *Goodbye, Columbus* had
brought its young author acclaim, Roth published his
first novel. A lengthy, serious book with an extensive
cast of characters and a complicated plot, *Letting Go*
is an ambitious attempt to explore the complexities of
various kinds of relationships. Its expansiveness, in
comparison with the brevity and sharp focus of *Goodbye, Columbus,* raises the idea that the book may
have represented for Roth a self-imposed trial of his
powers of invention. Whether or not he was attempting, in part, to test his ability to sustain a narrative
well beyond the boundaries of his previous fiction or
merely working within the space required for the un-
raveling of the drama of several lives, in *Letting Go*
Roth extends in detail some of the themes of the
novella and adds to them other concerns. In *Goodbye,
Columbus* the central focus was on the ambivalences
inherent in a young couple's romantic attachment,
but in *Letting Go* Roth presents the ambivalence inherent in many other kinds of relationships. Painting
now on a larger canvas, he reveals the attraction and
repulsion that exist in a father's love for his son and a
son's love for his father, in marriage, in friendship, and
in sexual affairs more beguiling than Neil Klugman's
simple lusts for Brenda Patimkin.

Out of such a pervasive treatment of human relationships, Roth raises first the crucial existential question of what it means to be a self and then follows it with an exploration of the impact of involvement with another, or others, upon the individual's sense of selfhood. Throughout the novel, as the characters' lives become enmeshed, Roth shows the confusion that erupts when involvement is taken for interference, commitment is regarded as constraint, autonomy is seen as detachment, and beneficence camouflages manipulation.

Realistically presented as complex human beings in need of preserving their personal existences and yet also in need of engagement with others, the major characters in *Letting Go* exemplify the modern dilemma of whether to find freedom and identity in involvement or in detachment. The title of *Letting Go* would seem to imply the answer: one finds freedom and selfhood in relinquishing claims upon others. The message of the novel is not, however, so clear-cut. While the book does reveal the destructiveness that can be done through "holding on," it also shows that in letting go the individual risks cutting himself adrift from moorings that lend stability. Although *Letting Go* seems to have more to say about the problems of relatedness than the solutions, it does imply that positive relationships can exist between the two destructive extremes of possessiveness and indifference. We may assume that such possibilities exist when a relationship is based upon a desire to preserve the integrity of both oneself and the other person. Almost without exception, however, Roth's novels demonstrate the unlikelihood that individuals caught between the demands of the self and the imperatives of another —be it father, mother, husband, wife, lover, friend, religion, or culture—can achieve this subtle balance.

In attempting a comprehensive representation of

the various manifestations and claims of love in *Letting Go*, Roth multiplies the possibility for demonstrating the complexities of human relationships by structuring two separate yet interwoven narratives. Functioning separately, each narrative involves sets of relationships that have their own particular characteristics; as the two narratives come together, a third dynamic is created out of the intermingling of the two separate stories and the interaction of the several characters.

At the center of both narratives is a young man attempting to "bully his way into manhood" by committing some decisive act that will validate him as a man and also allow him to do good—or be good. In the process, he struggles to learn his own nature by detaching himself from, or involving himself with, others. The secondary but certainly complementary figure in this trial of initiation into selfhood is the taciturn would-be novelist, Paul Herz, who marries a gentile girl at twenty because he is "fed up with being a boy" and spends the next several years attempting to deal with his estrangement from his Jewish parents. The primary character in this drama, and the central unifying consciousness in the novel, is Gabe Wallach, the independently wealthy son of a doting and possessive father, who finds it impossible to anchor his affections completely with any woman and who becomes entangled in the complicated lives of the Herzes. Around these two men, counterparts of one another in many ways, Roth establishes a panorama of relationships in which the participants obtrude upon and manipulate one another under the guise of love or duty.

In establishing a structure that accommodates and blends two narrative lines, Roth generally follows the technique of interweaving exposition of past events with the main line of action as he traces Gabe Wal-

lach's involvement with his father, Martha Reganhart,
and Paul and Libby Herz—the principal relationships
that test Gabe's idea of himself. The result is that
Gabe's past becomes a part of the dynamics of his
present. In depicting Paul Herz, however, Roth devotes a considerable segment of the novel to retro-
spective exposition, delineating Paul's love affair with
Libby, his conflict with his family when he ceases to
be their "good boy" and becomes their prodigal son,
and the deterioration that occurs in the marriage after
an unwanted pregnancy and an abortion. Consequently, by deferring most of the exposition of the past
until the novel is well under way, Roth is able to begin *in medias res* [9] and at a point at which both Gabe
Wallach and Paul Herz separately are already involved in relationships of conflict and irresolution.

The death of his mother has left Gabe the sole
object of his lonely and possessive father's attentions,
and he resists being overwhelmed by "parental benev-
olences" that seem to him calculated to absorb his
life. Paul, on the other hand, is estranged from his
family and entangled in a frustrating relationship with
his neurotic wife, Libby. Roth brings these two narrative skeins together early in the novel by having
Gabe and Paul, two displaced Jews from New York,
encounter one another in Iowa City, where both are
graduate students in English at the University of
Iowa. The independently wealthy Gabe finds himself
moved by the plight of the poverty-stricken Herzes
and strangely attracted to the enervated Libby. In a
way that has the appearance of kindness but actually seems to be an avoidance of coming to terms
with his life, Gabe finds himself attempting to "graft"
the Herzes to him. Both Libby and Paul respond to
Gabe's intrusion into their lives in ways that suggest
that they too view involvement with Gabe as a means
of escaping responsibility for solving their own prob-

lems of relationship. Libby progressively comes to think of Gabe as her potential rescuer from a husband whose sexual unresponsiveness frustrates her, and Paul partially wishes that Gabe would make love to his wife—or do something to "relieve us." Out of these various needs and inadequacies several other sets of relationship emerge, each colored by the other. There is the Gabe-Libby relationship, which is sexually tinged; there is the Gabe-Paul relationship, a kind of wary, watchful friendship that is at times warm and at others antagonistic; and there is the Gabe-Libby-Paul relationship, which forms the nexus of a set of conflicts that are central to the novel.

After Gabe leaves Iowa City and takes a teaching job at the University of Chicago, he manages to secure a position for Paul there as well. In inviting the Herzes back into his life, Gabe attempts to convince himself that he is motivated merely by the desire to do good for them, to "lift the Herzes up *into* life"; but it is apparent that after three years away from Iowa City and Paul and Libby, he is still afflicted with the same malaise that precipitated his first involvement with them.

In many ways, Gabe is a somewhat older version of Neil Klugman—directionless and indecisive; the boundaries of his personality seem "blurry and indefinite." But he is more self-analytical than Neil, and he suspects that by taking some decisive action he may discover his nature, formulate a distinct and definite identity. Apparently incapable of satisfactorily resolving his relationship with his father or becoming fully engaged in his relationship with his sometime lover Martha Reganhart, he turns to the needy Herzes to prove that he is capable of action. He focuses on the Herzes because by becoming involved in their lives, in "doing good" for them, he gains the feeling that he is participating in problems with manageable solutions. The Herzes need a car; he offers them one. Paul needs a decent teaching job; he arranges for him to have one. After Paul and Libby join him in Chicago, however, their problems become more personal and thus more complicated, and Gabe increasingly identifies their dilemmas with his own. Finally, after Libby persuades him to visit Paul's parents in Brooklyn and he undertakes her mission of relationship mending, Gabe has a moment of insight in which he realizes how susceptible he has been to Libby's manipulations: "There must be some weakness in men, I thought, (in Paul and myself, I later thought) that Libby wormed her way into."

Gabe's realization that the frail and often pathetic Libby uses her weaknesses to appeal to the protector in men and therefore make them conform to her wishes does not deter him from becoming even more engrossed in the Herzes' difficulties. He is no more capable of protecting Libby than the dutiful but unloving Paul; and yet when Libby, in a fit of temperament, declares that she wants a "baby or a dog or a TV" and explains that she is incapable of having a child, Gabe sets out like Sir Galahad to find the lady a baby to adopt. As he takes on the role of intermediary between the Herzes and Theresa Haug, the young mother of an illegitimate child, he increasingly views his ability to manipulate the process of adoption through to conclusion as a test of character. When it appears that Theresa's estranged husband, Harry Bigoness, will prevent the adoption by refusing to sign the necessary papers, Gabe attempts unsuccessfully to bribe him. Finally, obsessed with the idea that he must for once see something through to completion, Gabe loses his composure and the reserve that has continually kept him from acting decisively. Thinking that he has "passed beyond what he had kept normal by fortune and by strategy," he determines to act

even if doing so is imprudent. He returns to the Bigoness home with the baby, hoping he can elicit their
cooperation by appealing to their sympathy; but he
quickly becomes embroiled in a violent confrontation
that ends in his threatening to kill Bigoness and then
undergoing a total emotional collapse.

The novel ends with a letter from Gabe to Libby.
He has fled to London to recover from his breakdown,
to evaluate his past, and, perhaps, to begin anew. In
any event, he has removed himself from the en-
tanglement of the relationship with Libby and Paul
that had nearly engulfed him. If he has not achieved
the life of order and tenderness with another that he
had fantasized, at least as an exile he has come to
some conclusions concerning the nature of the man
who had wanted such an existence. Writing to Libby
about the night on which he risked uncharacteristic
impetuousness in his self-appointed task of arranging
the Herzes' lives, he calls it his "one decisive moment"
and suggests that to one who has "lived for a long
while as an indecisive man" such a moment is not
easily forgotten. The letter also indicates that Gabe
sees the wisdom of ending a relationship with the
Herzes that had in many ways been a mechanism
for avoiding self-examination and a substitute for
other, more apparently threatening relationships. Unlike Neil Klugman, who at the end of *Goodbye, Columbus* only contemplates his image in a glass, Gabe
Wallach deliberately undertakes the task of scrutiniz-
ing himself directly and attempting to make sense of
the "hook" he is on.

The novel ends as it begins, with a letter; and
the final letter, in which Gabe acknowledges the in-
sufficiencies of his character, both parallels and responds to the letter that opens the novel. The narrative that traces Gabe's interference in other people's
lives while he attempts to avoid too much intrusion

upon his own is introduced by a letter to Gabe from his dying mother. More than anything else, it is a death-bed confession of Mrs. Wallach's deficiencies of character and an acknowledgement that "whatever unhappiness has been in our family springs from me." She explains that she had always wanted to be "Very Decent to People," but she also indicates that the desire to be beneficent, or to be thought beneficent, can be a license to exert power and control.

The acknowledgment that destructiveness is often perpetrated under the self-righteous guise of "doing good" has significance not only for *Letting Go* but also for Roth's succeeding novels—in particular *When She Was Good* and *Portnoy's Complaint*. Mrs. Wallach establishes succinctly a major perspective in Roth's fiction about the relationship between apparent beneficence and manipulation when she says, "I was always doing things for another's good. The rest of my life I could push and pull at people with a clear conscience." In the two later novels, where the coercive power of the family becomes an even more central theme than it is in *Letting Go,* Roth shows directly the impact of the double message of goodness and control upon the susceptible offspring. Here, in *Letting Go,* the mother's letter hangs like a shadow over the relationships and events in Gabe's life, unobtrusively influencing what he avoids and what he seeks.

Out of his mother's admission that she was the powerful, destructive one in the family, that it was she who was always attempting to "improve [Gabe's father's] life for him, pushing, pulling," Gabe comes to fear intimacy both for what others might do to him and for what he might do to them. Consequently, he maintains a perilous balance; never being fully engaged himself, he becomes sufficiently involved in others' lives to interfere with them, only to withdraw at the first hint of intrusion upon his own life. While the source of this behavior may be traced to Gabe's interpretation of his mother's final message to him, the governing factor in the way he deals with relationships resides in his response to her letter—his vow to "do no violence to human life, not to another's, and not to my own."

On the surface a noble aim, this objective has disastrous results for Gabe. It leads him to recoil from loving and being loved by his father because he equates intimacy with the surrender of the self, of separateness. For much the same reason, it prevents him from sustaining a relationship with Martha Reganhart, the only person in the book sufficiently courageous and giving to offer him intimacy without subterfuge. Gabe himself acknowledges his propensity for avoiding the most threatening—and potentially most meaningful—relationships when he recognizes that "toward those for whom I felt no strong sentiment, I gravitated; where sentiment existed, I ran."

Construing love and commitment to mean principally a negation of the self in surrender to the other, Gabe thinks that by remaining detached he is eluding both pitfalls—manipulating like his mother or being manipulated like his father. From his childhood experience of being pulled between his parents, he sees in his mother and father only two prototypes for dealing with life and relationship, and he vows to succumb to neither extreme—to become neither the manipulator nor the manipulated. The irony, however, is that in seeking not to inflict or sustain violence, Gabe unwittingly recapitulates his mother's pattern of attempting to be "Very Decent to People," but without risking real involvement with them. He dabbles in the Herzes' lives with at least a conscious intention of "doing good" for them and because it provides him with a semblance of relationship without, apparently, entailing the commitment that a sustaining relationship with his father or with Martha would require of him. What he does not calculate as he intrudes upon Libby and Paul is the extent to which they too are manipulative; consequently, he becomes entangled in a three-sided liaison in which he and the Herzes "push and pull" at one another in an ultimately destructive fashion.

As he establishes Gabe at the center of two sets of relationships, with Paul and Libby on one side and Gabe's father and Martha Reganhart on the other, Roth principally explores the individual caught between two "wrong" ways of loving—one insufficient and the other controlling. In a scene that stands at a crucial point in the novel, when Gabe is most cut off from all his previous relationships and in a limbo of indecisiveness, Roth has Gabe recognize these two approaches as the extremes of impotence and savagery. The scene occurs after what Gabe calls a "rearrangement of people"—the "shufflings of parents and offspring"—has taken place. Gabe has finally established his independence from his father, and Mr. Wallach is about to assuage his loneliness by marrying a rather dull-witted widow with a penchant for alcohol; Gabe's affair with Martha has dissolved, and Martha has relinquished her children to her former husband; the Herzes have taken Theresa Haug's illegitimate child and are waiting to complete the adoption.

All of this "rearrangement" of lives has left Gabe feeling accountable for the impact he has had on others and yet impotent finally to make things right for those whom he, like his mother, has pushed and pulled and stood apart from. It is then that Roth allows Gabe (and the reader) a moment of insight into the dilemma that results when commitment is construed as an annihilation of the self and manipulation goes under the guise of beneficence. Contemplating the paths that have crossed his, Gabe realizes that

the same impulse that had led him to want to tidy up certain messy lives had led him also to turn his back upon others that threatened to engulf his own. He had finally come to recognize in himself a certain dread of the savageness of life. Tenderness, grace, affection: they struck him now as toys with which he had set about to hammer away at mountains. He had tried to be reasonable with everyone—but the demands made upon him had been made by unreasonable people. But the demands made on *them* had not been reasonable. Still, he had tried to be true to his feelings, to what he was. . . . So on the one hand he still believed himself put upon; on the other, he saw—or was willing to see—where he had not been savage enough. And he doubted that he ever could be, for it did not seem that he knew how to be; and he was not finally sure that he should be. Or *had* he been savage? Circles. . . .

It is his view that love is violent and life savage that causes Gabe to want to protect himself from others and to "do good" for them from an emotional distance; but he comes to see, however vaguely, that complete detachment is impossible.

It is not until the end of the novel, however, that Gabe realizes the delicate balance that exists between involvement and interference. Consequently, out of a need to prove that he is capable of acting decisively, of carrying through with his plan to "tidy up" the complicated lives of the Herzes, he launches himself into a crusade to overcome every obstacle in the way of the adoption.

Gabe's obsession with facilitating the Herzes' adoption of a child is, then, on one level his trial of initiation, his attempt to "bully his way into manhood" by proving to himself that he can exert power for a good cause. He also comes to recognize through the process his own desire for paternity. At one point, standing over the baby Rachael in her crib, Gabe considers the possibility of fatherhood and envisions it as a demarcation between young manhood and maturity: "Till now everything had been by way of initiation. Bumbling toward a discovery of his nature, he had made the inevitable errors of a young man. But he was ready now to be someone's husband, someone's father."

From another perspective, Gabe's determination to risk the savagery he so dreads is an act of penance for the guilt he feels for having deprived his father of a son and even some vague guilt for the death of Martha Reganhart's son. Indeed, most of the relationships in the novel deal in one way or another with "letting go" of children: Mr. Wallach ceases to grasp at Gabe and settles for the widow; Paul and Libby are both deserted by their parents and choose to abort a child they cannot easily afford; Martha Reganhart lets her children go to their father; and Theresa Haug relinquishes her child to the Herzes. It is no wonder that Gabe comes to view the Herzes' adoption of Rachael as the "crystallization of several acts in one." All the relinquishing of children that takes place in the novel is symbolically counterbalanced only by the one act of restoration in which Gabe takes part; consequently, Gabe's participation in this symbolic act takes on overwhelming significance for him.

Ironically, the adoption seems to have for Paul Herz, the adoptive father, little of the significance it has for Gabe. There is no indication that he views this "rearrangement of lives" as anything more than an appeasement for Libby. That it has so little significance for him may be, in part, because he has already solved to his own satisfaction the question of paternity and the sacrifice that is involved in father-son relationships. Paul comes to understand and accept his relationship with his father in a moment of revelation at the cemetery as his father is being buried. He comprehends for the first time the elemental unity of father and son and feels himself to be "under a wider beam." With the death of his father, Paul seems to let go of the guilt and sense of recrimination with which he had lived since his marriage to Libby and also to relinquish some of his illusions about himself and the world around him. From that point on, he distances himself progressively from Libby, assumes a fatherly stance when he encounters her, and considers his youth a thing of the past. He reaches the manhood that he had so desired at twenty, but it is a listless maturity, without joy or optimism.

By the end of the novel, both Gabe Wallach and Paul Herz have, each in his own way, severed connections. After the tempestuous early years of his marriage to Libby and the death of his father, Paul realizes that it is possible "no longer to have any connection to anybody," and he opts for emotional disengagement from his wife and family. During the process of the novel, Gabe achieves independence from his father, severs his relationship with Martha Reganhart, and, by the end of the novel, frees himself from attachments to the Herzes. Each finally sees himself as a "man," but the achievement is without the anticipated fulfillment. For Gabe, however, who sets for himself the task of making sense of the bonds that hold him, there is hope. Unlike Paul, he realizes that despite his attempts to become the autonomous self, claims are always made upon the individual and freedom does not consist in alienation but in resolving those claims.

In turning from the somewhat whimsical treatment of selfhood and relationship in *Goodbye, Columbus* to a more serious and expanded handling of the theme in *Letting Go*, Roth relies for both style and subject on the influence of Henry James.[10] In the early pages of the novel, he follows James in his stylistic restraint and establishes James's *The Portrait of a Lady* as a touchstone, a point of reference, through which he adds texture to his exploration of relationship and manipulation. With a stroke of calculated irony, he has Gabe place between the pages of *The Portrait of a Lady* his mother's confession of lifelong "benevolent" manipulation so that the parallel can be drawn between her and Isabel Archer, the "pushy" protagonist of James's novel. Roth also employs James as a kind of shorthand device for revealing some of the attributes of his own characters. Gabe, for example, cannot wholeheartedly condemn Isabel Archer's manipulativeness because he associates her with his mother. Libby, on the other hand, both romanticizes her and condemns her manipulative use of power. But Martha Reganhart, who is less concerned with being decorous than Gabe and more sensible about love than Libby, reacts with distaste to James's "virginal mind."

At the end of the novel, Gabe's exile to London and the stance he takes toward life are deliberately designed to evoke the restrained but intellectually involved Jamesian "American in Europe." From the advantage of this distanced perspective, Gabe begins to consider the attachments of his young manhood; and while the boundaries of his personality may be only slightly more distinct than before, they now have expanded to incorporate his one venture into the psychological unknown. He values the moment when, having acted with uncharacteristic impetuosity, he let go of that propensity for keeping a "crafty rule over [his] responses" bequeathed to him by his mother and acted without strategy; and in the dissolution of the self he has known, he sets himself the task of "making sense" of a potentially new identity.

As Roth's first extended fictional effort, *Letting Go* serves as an early indication that, despite shifts in tone, technique, and scope, there is a basic thematic continuity to Roth's work. The novel expands and plays variations on the theme of individual determination versus social and familial coerciveness that the previous short stories and the novella had introduced. Furthermore, it anticipates Roth's next two novels, *When She Was Good* and *Portnoy's Complaint,* not only in its emphasis on the family as a particularly powerful force but also in its ironic examination of the idea of being or doing "good." Most of Roth's fiction, in one way or another, turns the concept of "good" around as one might a kaleidoscope, to reveal a changed pattern in each new position.[11] In the short stories and in *Goodbye, Columbus,* Roth's concern with what it means to be "good" is implied in the equation that Rabbi Binder, Goldie Epstein, the secular Jewish community of Woodenton, and Mr. and Mrs. Patimkin make between the necessity for conforming and being good, normal, or sane. Ozzie Freedman's questioning and defiance are considered by his mother and Rabbi Binder as "bad"; Goldie Epstein considers Lou Epstein's adultery abnormal; Eli Peck is regarded as insane by his friends when he identifies with a manifestation of Jewishness they consider undesirable; and the Patimkin parents are puzzled when "good" daughter Brenda repays their generosity with "bad" behavior. In *Letting Go,* Roth shifts the perspective and forms another and new pattern that deals with goodness—this time focusing explicitly on "doing good." Mrs. Wallach's final letter to Gabe establishes at the beginning of the novel a connection between doing good and manipulation and between being good and coercion. During the course of the novel, Gabe shows himself to be his mother's son as he interferes in the lives of others with the notion that he is "doing things" for their good.

When She Was Good

In the fiction subsequent to *Letting Go* and in works as different in tone and intent as *Our Gang* and *My Life as a Man*, Roth continues to examine the various uses and misuses of the concept of goodness. But it is in *When She Was Good* and *Portnoy's Complaint*, the two novels that immediately follow *Letting Go*, that Roth gives the sharpest focus to the ironies inherent in being and doing good and shows the fine line that exists between true beneficence and destructiveness and between self-determination and behaving according to another's standard. In these two novels, doing good often comes to mean manipulation or destructiveness, and being good often represents acquiescent conformity to the wishes of those who have defined "good."

Perhaps more obviously than any other of Roth's novels, *When She Was Good* and *Portnoy's Complaint* dramatize what Roth sees as the "problematical nature of moral authority and of social restraint and regulation"; and in each instance, the problem arises out of a conflict between the individual and the family. Reacting to the constraints placed upon her by her family under the guise of good, of protection, Lucy Nelson in *When She Was Good* becomes the "horrid" little girl implied in the poem from which Roth draws the title of the book. In seeking to resist the moral authority of his family, Alexander Portnoy becomes the lustful Jewish "bad" boy. Roth makes no attempt to excuse either of his protagonists for their outrageous behavior since neither excusing nor condemning is the point of either novel. Instead, both books explore the problems that result when the desire for personal autonomy comes up against the restraints of the family, from which the individual needs both autonomy and sanction. Different as these novels are in their outward trappings, they are similar in that the central conflict in both involves "bad," defiant offspring and their protective, coercive families.

Although the general critical tendency has been to see *When She Was Good* and *Portnoy's Complaint* as opposites, Roth often links the two together in comments on his work. In a piece written in 1969 in response to a review of *Portnoy's Complaint* by Diana Trilling, Roth offers an extended analysis of the similarities between the two books, saying that any "alert reader" can see that both are preoccupied with the "warfare between parents and children." He adds that although the books are "wholly antithetic in cultural and moral orientation," in each the protagonist assumes the stance of the self-righteous and enraged offspring. It is in this context that he calls Lucy Nelson and Alexander Portnoy "soul mates" and says that they are "in their extreme resentment and disappointment, like the legendary unhappy children out of two familiar American family myths." In one myth the Jewish son feels persecuted by the seductive mother, and in the other the gentile daughter feels betrayed by her alcoholic father. The environments are different, but the protagonists' reactions are the same—"rage as well as a sense of loss and nostalgia."

Later, Roth reiterates the connection between *When She Was Good* and *Portnoy* by suggesting that Lucy's and Portnoy's rage against "long-standing authorities believed . . . to have misused their power" actually functions as the primary oppressor of each of them. That oppressive rage, however, grows out of family situations in which the protagonists perceive themselves to be caught in a double bind, or a conflict between two mutually exclusive goods. It is not a particularly abnormal situation: parents offer love, protection, and approval in return for acquiescence; children want love and approval without having to surrender their fledgling identities. The conflict is intensified by guilt and recrimination, and the children end up defying the parents and trying to live with some moral structure of their own devising. It is, Roth suggests, a "familiar American family myth."

In *When She Was Good*, however, Roth explores the myth with deadly seriousness, and the result is a drama of family destructiveness unrelieved by the comedy of *Portnoy's Complaint* and tragic in its implications. Leaving the familiar territory of Jewish families, Roth focuses on a family evocative of American typicality. It is geographically midwestern, religiously Protestant, economically middle class, and afflicted with more than a touch of banality. For all its "goyish" flavor, however, the novel is not disconnected thematically from Roth's previous fiction; and even some of the characterological traits of its heroine are to be found in one of Roth's earlier "shikses," [12] Libby Herz, the dissatisfied gentile wife in *Letting Go*. Lucy Nelson, the anti-heroine of *When She Was Good*, recalls Libby Herz in her ability to detect and use the vulnerability of men against them; and because by the end of the novel she has become an avenging tyrant, Lucy has often been characterized in one epigrammatic phrase: a self-righteous, ball-breaking bitch.

Actually, Lucy is the tragic victim of a social milieu and a family construct that literally drive her insane. Striving for self-determination, she is caught in a social environment that is based on the patriarchal concept of the male as protector and of the female as protected vassal, and in a family in which the males who purport to protect are powerless to do so. Such an arrangement requires a great deal of complicity from the women as well as the men to sustain these protector-protected roles and to pretend that they represent reality. Relentless in her dedication to the truth as she sees it, Lucy refuses to participate in the pretense that the men in her family are capable protectors and, therefore, to relinquish her will to them. She is finally driven to madness by her ability to see but not rectify the fallacies involved in this "protection racket" that operates in her family to impose one of the most effective and destructive double-bind situations to be found in any of Roth's fictional families. In a very real sense, Lucy is destroyed by love, or rather by violence masquerading as love.

On the surface, the dynamics of the double bind in Lucy Nelson's family are relatively simple: the stability of the family depends on the perpetuation of the lie that Lucy's grandfather, Willard Carroll, can protect its members from misfortune if they will rely on him and relinquish their own volition. The more accurate oppositional message, which Lucy perceives even as a child, is that Willard fails completely in his attempts to be the family protector. The context that explains the apparent necessity for the double bind is not, however, simple. It is a context larger than the nuclear family, since Willard's influence extends not only to his wife and daughter but also to his son-in-law and granddaughter; it is, further, a context that necessitates an understanding of the forces that shaped Willard Carroll. The idea that the sins of the fathers are visited on the children becomes actualized in Roth's depiction of the way in which each family provides the basis for a succeeding generation's destruction.

Early in his boyhood Willard's sensibilities are aggrieved by the illiteracy and savagery of his rural family. When his infant sister Ginny suffers an attack of scarlet fever that leaves her retarded, his parents' insensitivity creates in Willard an obsession for establishing a "civilized" family, one that he can insulate from brutality and pain. When Willard leaves "Iron City," it is to settle in a town called, not coincidentally, Liberty Center, which he sees in idyllic terms of calm, beauty, and order and envisions as a place where he can be "free at last of that terrible tyranny of cruel men and cruel nature."

Once established in an environment seen as conducive to the realization of his dream, Willard sets out to implement his ideal. He finds a wife, secures a job, has a daughter, acquires a house, and proceeds to establish a life of relationship based on his misguided and ultimately destructive notion of what constitutes a civilized family. Ironically, his version of that ideal of freedom imposes a tyranny of love as he attempts to protect everyone in his family from the savagery that in his past has been symbolized by the maiming of "poor little Ginny."

Willard comes to relate to every member of his family as he has to the retarded Ginny. He sees them as unable to protect themselves, and, attempting to mitigate his boyhood feelings of impotence over Ginny's sickness, he takes on the role of protector for them all. It is significant that Willard often thinks of the other members of the family in ways that recall his sister. When his daughter Myra, for example, is well into her thirties, Willard compares her to Ginny and sees her as pathetically weak, with thin little wrists and ankles and fragile little feet. He also thinks of Duane, his drunken, ineffectual son-in-law, in terms of his afflicted sister and is moved to absolve him from responsibility for his weaknesses because of the sudden realization that *"there is nothing the man can do. He is afflicted with himself. Like Ginny."*

It is even more ironic that Willard, in his failure

to recognize human separateness, is himself like Ginny. In her dementia, the grown Ginny becomes so confused over identity that she thinks Lucy is an extension of herself. Willard finally has to place her in an institution because, as he phrases it, "she could not understand the most basic fact of human life, that I am me and you are you." Yet out of his desire to do what he believes to be good for others, Willard himself disregards this basic fact. Lucy, Myra, Duane, and Willard's wife, Berta, are all treated as if they were mere extensions of Willard himself. Out of love, he attempts to assume ultimate responsibility for them; but his is the manipulative love of the "do-gooder," the person who, like Mrs. Wallach in *Letting Go*, wants to be "Very Decent to People" and masks control with beneficence. Willard views everyone in his family as fragile, and, wanting to protect them all, he cannot or will not allow those he loves to take the risks inherent in being independent persons, separate from himself. Failing to understand basic human individuality, as his sister had, he deprives those whom he attempts to protect of their essential identity.

Only in Lucy, his granddaughter, does Willard encounter a challenge to his carefully constructed image of himself as family protector. In one key scene, Lucy takes it upon herself to act and calls the police to arrest her drunken father. Willard becomes indignant because her action threatens not only his idea of the civilized family but also his sense of himself as the only one in the family with the right or ability to act. When Willard questions Lucy repeatedly about why she called the police rather than him to make her father "stop," she responds in a way that indicates she has seen the truth behind the facade of his alleged protection: "Because you can't. . . . Well . . . you don't."

Faced with Lucy's realization that he is less effectual in solving family crises than he pretends to be, Willard protests that he is not, after all, God or Jesus Christ. This is a technique to which Willard resorts time and again when he is caught between the reality of his impotence to protect and the necessity of clinging to his illusion of efficacy within the family. His protest is in actuality a defensive maneuver that allows him to claim the role of protector, to absolve himself when his protection fails, and to continue preventing others from functioning autonomously. Willard has power—the power to arrange other people's lives—but only so long as his family remains powerless, dependent upon him.

Lucy's self-directed action threatens the unspoken family contract, which says that everyone who conforms to Willard's notion of passivity and weakness will be protected by him and "loved" by the whole family. Lucy violates the code of acquiescence that controls her family, and Willard attempts to coerce her into conformity through guilt. In the previous scene and in a subsequent scene in which Lucy locks her father out of the house, Willard reprimands her for being an ungrateful, deluded child whose rebelliousness will bring the family to destruction. Whichever way she turns, Lucy *has* to feel guilty—thus the insidious nature of the double bind. If she restores the family to a sense of reality, she will destroy the mystique that holds it together. But if she leaves the family as it is, Myra will continue to be the helpless, victimized wife of an irresponsible husband; Berta, Lucy's grandmother, will always protest vainly against Willard's ineffectual protectiveness; and Willard will forever assert his omnipotence. Lucy, therefore, is "bad" if she acts and "good" if she submits to the destructive lie.

Later, other men will use similar methods to control Lucy and to imply that she is not only bad but insane when she attempts to act according to her sense of reality, which, not surprisingly, becomes distorted. Conditioned by repeated experiences in which she "can't win," in which action causes guilt and inaction is intolerable, in which men assert protection and do not protect, Lucy becomes the "ball-breaking bitch," turning on the weakness disguised as power that she sees in her grandfather, in her father, and finally in all men—and becoming not only the oppressor of others but, as Roth has said, her own worst enemy.

As an adolescent and young woman, Lucy makes several limited attempts to establish an autonomy that will free her from the destructive psychology of her family. In one of these efforts she turns to the Catholic church, hoping it will effect a change in her father and relieve her of the guilt of hating him. With the example of Saint Teresa of Lisieux placed constantly before her, however, she learns the message of patient suffering rather than assertive action. Both the religious and the secular implications of Saint Teresa's "It is for us to console Our Lord, not for him to be consoling us" seem to indicate that neither Jesus Christ nor Willard Carroll may be expected to intervene significantly on her behalf. Her experiment with Catholicism and its doctrines of acquiescence lasts only until the efficacy of faith is tested:

So Lucy dedicated herself to a life of submission, humility, silence and suffering; until the night her father pulled down the shade and up-ended the pan of water in which her mother was soaking her beautiful, frail feet. After calling upon Saint Teresa of Lisieux and Our Lord—and getting no reply—she called the police.

Rejecting the church's ineffectiveness and Saint Teresa's "suffering little guts," Lucy asserts her own perception of the truth and right to action: "I am right and they are wrong and I will not be destroyed!"

Ironically, she is destroyed by the strength, turned to rigidity, that might have saved her. In an attempt to preserve her identity by claiming exclusive rights to truth, Lucy falls into the schizoid trap inherent in her family situation. Her growing detachment and claim to judgmental superiority result finally in an inability to be reconciled to reality.

Lucy's final attempt to extricate herself from the constrictions of the family bind is represented in her sexual involvement with and marriage to Roy Bassart. Each step of the relationship, from the seduction to the separation that culminates in Lucy's suicide, provides a gauge to Lucy's mental decline. Roth makes it clear that the seduction, for example, is more symptomatic of Lucy's confusion over truth and trust than of Roy's adeptness at persuasion. Roy's approach, amateurish as it is, succeeds because it equates love with trust and trust with truth. These are the qualities Lucy has seen distorted in her own home, where Willard, Duane, and Myra all lie to her as they ask her to trust them. But by this point, Lucy is unable to deal with communication in a "normal" fashion by interpreting levels of truth. In her increasingly rigid view of reality, Lucy finds everything to be either absolutely true or absolutely false and consequently cannot cope with the equivocations in Roy's technique. Their conversation is illustrative:

". . . But what if you don't like me? Really? How can I know you're telling the truth?"

"I told you *I don't lie!*"

When she didn't respond, he came closer to her.

"You say love," Lucy said. "But you don't mean love."

"I get carried away, Lucy. That's not a lie. I get carried away, by the mood. I like music, so it affects me. So that's not a 'lie.' "

What had he just said? She couldn't even understand.

Lucy does not comprehend that in this exchange Roy is walking a kind of communication tightrope that redefines love as sex-sentiment. Since she is not capable of responding to the complexity of the message, she submits to his "trust me, trust me," which paradoxically represents the commitment she most needs and the distortion with which she is most familiar. Lucy has been conditioned to see in men's insistence on trust the promise of protection and, simultaneously, an incapacity for making good that promise. Yet she continues to hope for, and half believe in, its fulfillment.

Lucy's ambivalence indicates that despite her determination to be independent of the family violence, that pattern is already established as the prototype for her reactions. By now she has no capacity for action untinged by the influence of her conditioning, and in the last half of the novel she plays out at different times one or the other of the two alternative roles she has derived from her family. In her reaction to the doctor who confirms her pregnancy, she assumes the "female" attitude of one in need of protection by a male and pleads with him to "save her life." When he refuses to act his part and keep her safely within the closure of the double bind—the only security she knows—Lucy turns once more to the members of her family and tries to force them into making the myth of family protection come true by relinquishing her will to them: "Lucy closed her eyes. Why hadn't she done this at the start? Just gotten into bed and left it all to them. Wasn't that what they were always wanting to be, her family?" Lucy demonstrates here the irony of the "can't win" situation, which she has experienced so repeatedly that although she is sane enough to see its fallacy, she is not sane enough to free herself from it. Consequently,

she must try to perpetrate the only reality she knows
—the reality of the lie.

It becomes obvious that her family is incapable
of any action effectual in solving the problem of her
pregnancy, and Lucy is stunned into realizing that
her "predicament was *real*. It was no plot she had
invented to bring them all to their senses. . . . And
it was not going to disappear either, just because
somebody besides herself was at long last taking it
seriously. It was real!" When the role of acquiescence
does not work, Lucy turns to the alternative of her
family model and assumes the Willard-like stance of
protector-controller. Determined not to make her
mother's mistakes, she makes Willard's. Upon marrying Roy and establishing her own family, Lucy resorts
to the only techniques she knows to facilitate the
survival of the family—control, destructive protection,
manipulation, and, paradoxically in view of her obsession with truth, lies.

The earliest indication that Lucy's alternatives for
response are limited to emulating either Myra or
Willard appears when she contemplates ending the
affair with Roy. After vowing to break off with him,
she finds she cannot carry through with her decision
because it might cause him to give up his plans to
go to art school and pursue a career in photography:
"But that was his affair, not hers. . . . Or was it? . . .
It might even mean his whole career. Because he
depended on her—he listened to her—he loved her.
Roy loves me." Here, despite the one clear-sighted
observation that it is Roy's affair and not hers, Lucy
is following a set of roles that have been established
by Myra and Willard. She imitates the hated model
of Myra, who does anything for her husband just because he is weak and "sweet" and loves her. But even
worse, she is beginning to see Roy (and treat him)
much as Willard sees Duane and Myra: he is too

weak and ineffectual to live his life without her direction and control; therefore, she must provide that
control.

By the fourth year of their marriage, Lucy and
Roy are enmeshed in a complex situation. She controls
through thinking that she has the responsibility for
making him into a man, and he copes with her confused view of reality by pretending to be what she
wants him to be. Yet Lucy can stand neither the truth
nor the pretense:

She saw him pretending now nearly all the time, so as to
avoid the clashes that had taken place almost weekly
after the first six months of the marriage. Every time he
opened his mouth she could hear that he did not mean a
single word, but was trying only to disarm her by saying
what he thought she wanted him to say. He would do
anything now to avoid a battle, anything but really change.

The change Lucy wants is impossible for Roy to
effect because it contains too many conflicting elements. She wants Roy to fulfill her conception of a
man, yet her need for security requires that she be
the director of a family of dependent weaklings; she
wants him to provide an honest relationship, full of
trust and truth, but he must conform to her version
of truth. Finally, Lucy becomes both victim and vil-
lain. As the progeny of a double-bind family, she re-
enacts its pattern. Because her experience has been
destroyed, she becomes the destroyer of the experience of others in order to salvage what she can of her
own identity.

Lucy's victimization is all the more complete because even as she takes on the destructive God-like
image characteristic of Willard, she senses, but cannot
fully comprehend, the fallacy in her omnipotence.
Contemplating her relationship to her son, she reveals
her ambivalence: "Here he is. I saved his life. I did

it—all alone. Oh, why should I feel such misery? Why is my life like this?" Unlike the totally schizophrenic individual, Lucy is too closely tied to the realities on both sides of the bind to be able to free herself into another world. Caught in a preschizophrenic state, she clings to a vision of this world that isolates her but does not project her out of reality altogether. She maintains her absolutist view of truth and becomes enraged when she cannot hold her family together with it. Describing herself in terms indicative of a god who creates, controls, and saves, she shouts in frustration at Roy's attempt to act independently, "You can't be saved. You don't even want to be." Later, in her last encounter with her mother, she adds the quality of judgment to her God-like attributes. She tells Myra that her father has stayed away from home for four years because "he is terrified of my judgment."

Lucy now begins to demonstrate not only the confusion but also the delusion of the schizoid. Finally, in the crisis that comes at the home of Roy's uncle Julian, where many previously unspoken truths are verbalized, she begins to glimpse the "real truth" that her rigidity has obscured. As a consequence of being forced to confront the reality of her destructiveness to Roy and her son, she "lets go" into a schizophrenic escape. One image, appearing twice, heralds her into that other world: she has a vision of her father sitting in a prison with "INNOCENT" written in lipstick on his teeth. It is as if all her duplicity and condemnation have crystallized into the one truth that is later enunciated by Father Damrosch in Lucy's hallucinatory dream. She asks, "Why can't people be good?" and finally he answers, "The world is imperfect. . . . Because we are weak, we are corrupt. Because we are sinners. Evil is the nature of mankind." She realizes that her father is a victim too, and that she must share the guilt for making him one. She and her father inhabit the same imperfect world, and she is neither so good nor he so bad as she had believed.

Lucy's death, with the added symbolism of her father's letter frozen to her face, follows her recognition that Duane is human and therefore innocent and forgivable. Her dying is undeniably suicidal. For Lucy to take the step into autonomous being would mean acting on the realization that neither she nor anyone else can be the god who controls another's reality; it would mean rejecting the pattern offered by the protective family and giving up the pretense both of protecting and of being protected. Unfortunately, because Lucy no longer has the flexibility such self-determining action requires, the materialization of an alternative that is independent of her past experience threatens her very existence. The details of her death are symbolic: frozen into rigidity, Lucy is caught in a posture that suggests she is warding off a blow.

This devastating picture of the dynamics of the American family, which destroys under the guise of protection, appropriately depicts the woman as the primary victim of the "protection racket." Outside the novel, in the world of social and familial realities, the protector-protected roles exist and are maintained. In his portrayal of the violence and invalidation of experience that characterize the families in this novel, Roth demonstrates that the woman who plays the protected "feminine" role can never achieve the full potential of her humanity. Paradoxically, neither can the woman who adopts the "masculine" role of protector, for even as Lucy emasculates her husband, she wants to make him into a "man." Thus, no one can "win" in the family without a reinterpretation of the myth that assigns limited and unrealistic roles to the two sexes.

Throughout the novel, Lucy expresses confusion

and resentment toward the roles and the fact that no one can play them "right." Furthermore, she has no models from whom to learn any way of breaking out of the role-bind conflict. Her mother is a hopelessly dependent daddy's baby who destroys her own and her husband's possibilities for maturity by refusing to leave the protection of her father's home. Willard remembers Myra as a girl, always "practicing something feminine: crocheting, music, poetry. There were times when it seemed to him as though nothing in the world could so make a man want to do good in life as the sight of a daughter's thin little wrists and ankles." Myra, remaining the fragile little girl her father sees her as, continues to play all the feminine roles assigned to her until, by the end of the book, she becomes a parody of the whimpering child she has always been.

Berta, Lucy's grandmother, is a more genuinely tragic figure than Myra because, like Lucy, she can see the consequences of Willard's protection. Berta tries repeatedly to tell her husband that grown children should be allowed to live their own lives; but because she has accepted all the ramifications of her role as wife, she simply verbalizes the reality of the situation and then allows Willard to continue with his dishonest protectiveness. Her refusal to act enrages Lucy, who needs an ally to help her break out of the restrictive pattern of the family. In their incapacities, Myra and Berta mark two points on the continuum that defines women in the novel: Myra perceives none of the realities of the family situation and therefore cannot act; Berta sees but will not act. In a further progression, Lucy has both clarity of perception and the will to act, but the family contrivance to make her feel guilty and, ultimately, nullify her action frustrates her to the point where she becomes destructive and finally is destroyed.

As Lucy plays out her two opposing roles and the novel reaches its conclusion with an intensification of conflict, Roth shows the relationships nurtured in the modern family to be totally destructive of the possibility of communication between men and women. The men hate the women and see them as castraters because they do not accept the male as a god, and the women hate the men for not being the protective gods that the family myth says they are. Some of the last speeches by Roy, Julian, and Lucy make the rage and separation between the sexes quite clear. When, for example, Lucy finally realizes the irreconcilable nature of her conflict, she directs her anger first at Roy for his inability to fulfill her expectations of what a man is supposed to be:

"You worm! Don't you have any guts at all? Can't you stand on your own two feet, *ever?* You sponge! You leech! You weak, hopeless, spineless, coward! You'll never change —you don't even *want* to change! You don't even know what I *mean* by change! You stand there with your dumb mouth open! Because you have no backbone! None!"

"La Voy's not the pansy, Roy. You are."

Next, Lucy directs her frustration at Willard, the source of the dishonest communication in her family:

"Please," she said to her grandfather, *"please do not interfere.* You are not capable of understanding what is going on. You are an impotent and helpless man. You always were and you still are, and if it weren't for you, none of this might have begun in the first place. So please, leave this to *me!"*

Finally, Lucy castigates a system larger than her family and rejects the whole sex that her grandfather and husband represent:

She would be mother and father to them both, and so the three of them—herself, her little boy, and soon her little girl too—would live without cruelty, without treachery, without betrayal; yes without men. Yes, goodbye, goodbye, brave and stalwart men. Goodbye, protectors and defenders, heroes and saviors. You are no longer needed, you are no longer wanted—alas, you have been revealed for what you are. Farewell, farewell, philanderers and frauds, cowards and weaklings, cheaters and liars. Fathers and husbands, farewell!

At last, and for once, Lucy is saying exactly what she means. Men promised to protect, save, and defend her; they have not done it. Now they can all go to hell.

The comments late in the book by Roy and Julian demonstrate the same polarization of attitudes against women that Lucy reveals toward men. If women cannot carry out the roles required by the family myth, they too will be rejected. Roy, who is never as violent as Lucy, nevertheless reveals his attitude toward her unwillingness to assume the role of the long-suffering support for a man whom she pretends to see as God. The names he hurls at her when he leaves with their son reveal his bitterness toward a wife whose opposition exposes his immaturity and weakness: she is hateful, bossy, and heartless. Roy's uncle Julian is much more specific in his denunciation of Lucy as a castrating female who must be stopped by the man with the toughest balls, and his speeches closely approximate Lucy's in revealing the irreconcilable schism in communication between men and women.

"Oh," said Julian, "you are a real saint, you are."

"We have all taken enough orders and insults from this little bitch here—"

"Because that's all you are, you know. A little ball-breaker of a bitch. That's the saint you are, kiddo—Saint Ball-Breaker. And the world is going to know it, too, before I'm through with you."

"The busting of the balls stops with these. That's right, you smile through your tears, you smile how smart you are and what a terrible mouth old Julian has. . . . But . . . you busted his [Roy's] balls, and you were starting in on little Eddie's, but that is *all* over."

The impasse here is one that follows naturally from the pattern of false communication on which the relationships between the men and women in the families have been established. Julian, a "normal" man, can feel relatively comfortable in asserting his "masculinity" against a woman whom he perceives to have abandoned her designated role. Lucy, however, now has the prototype for no role other than those which she has already played; and, with the complicity of the women who have sacrificed themselves to "protection," the husbands and fathers succeed in nullifying Lucy's existence as she in her madness can only wish to nullify theirs.

Roth offers no hope in this, his most pessimistic portrayal of the family, for the establishment of a positive ground of communication between men and women. He shows the impetus for control in both men and women to be embedded in their vulnerability, and he locates the genesis of misguided patterns of relationship in the interplay between cultural, familial, and personal forces. It is in presenting accurately the complexities inherent in human relationships rather than in posing solutions that Roth's achievement lies; and the artistic, and ultimately moral, success of the novel consists in its providing a basis for understanding the conditions out of which individual behavior originates.

Like a dramatist conforming to the Aristotelian conventions of probability,[13] Roth concentrates in *When She Was Good* on showing cause and effect so that the audience can understand why Willard is obsessed with his family's being "civilized" or why

Lucy is frustrated with men's weaknesses. Yet it is characteristic of Roth's artistic vision that he seeks neither to exonerate those who act as they do largely because of family or cultural circumstance nor to condemn them because they confuse protection and possessiveness, love and violence, ethical duty and self-righteousness. In *When She Was Good,* for example, in which these confusions are manifested in the extreme, Roth avoids moral categorizing by showing Willard and Lucy in particular to be not only the perpetrators of destructiveness in the family but its victims as well.

Roth softens the picture of Willard Carroll's destructive kind of love by showing the difference between intention and effect in Willard's mode of relationship with his family. Like many of Roth's characters whose influence shapes the destiny of others, Willard wants to do good for those he considers to be in his care. His intentions are humane and charitable, yet the effect of his mode of relationship with the members of his family renders all except Lucy weak and dependent upon him. This gives him substantial control over their lives, but it also makes him, in turn, a proper scapegoat for their own lack of courage.

It is in the portrayal of Lucy, however, that Roth best reveals his capacity for providing the rationales for behavior that offer a basis for sympathetic understanding of the character. Lucy is presented as horrid in her anger and pathetic in her desire to love and be loved; but, above all, in terms of the objectivity with which Roth depicts her, she is understandable as the combined product of the family that produced her and of a nature less tractable than any other in the Carroll-Nelson household. The victim of her father's adolescent irresponsibility and her grandfather's responsible ineffectuality, Lucy turns into an obstinate, self-righteous virago out of her will to survive the disorder of her family and her desire for moral integrity. Just as Willard wants to do good, so Lucy wants to be good; but by the end of the novel, she is possessed with a mad, messianic fervor not only to be good but to make everyone else conform to her notion of morality. Willard forgives every weakness; Lucy forgives none. It is perhaps the principal irony of the novel that in their attempts to do good and be good, Lucy and Willard affect the lives about them disastrously. "The world is imperfect," preaches Father Damrosch near the end of the novel, and this constitutes a substantial portion of Roth's message. He shows that even in Liberty City modes of relationship based on the best intentions can have disastrous consequences.

In general, critics have failed to recognize the stylistic and thematic sophistication of *When She Was Good* and have relegated it to the position of a kind of "Gentile Experiment" by a writer who is at his best when writing in the "Jewish vernacular." That Roth can achieve verisimilitude in the presentation of character, setting, cultural mores, and language when he ventures away from the familiar Jewish culture of the East Coast and into the "foreign" territory of gentile heartland America is, in fact, a tribute to his versatility and the accuracy of his "ear" for more than one kind of vernacular. Roth suggests in one of his interviews that his artistic intention in *When She Was Good* was to "make a correct presentation of the problem" by making the language and tone of the novel consonant with the characters and the milieu he was depicting. He indicates that he wanted to communicate by his characters' "way of saying things, their way of seeing things and judging them." Consequently, the restrained style and the lack of obscenity and sexual explicitness are appropriate presentations of the problem in *When She Was Good*, just as the stylistic excesses, obscenity, and sexual frankness are central to the issue in *Portnoy's Complaint,* the novel in which Roth discarded the sobriety of *Letting Go* and *When She Was Good.*

Portnoy's Complaint

The issue in *Portnoy's Complaint* is how Alexander Portnoy, the good little Jewish son of Jake and Sophie Portnoy, can be as "bad" as he wants to be and also be free of guilt. The point of the novel is that Portnoy can be neither. For all his defiance of parental and cultural taboos, which he tries to express through sexual excess and verbal obscenity, he can never be bad enough to be liberated from the proscriptions of his upbringing. His masturbation, lasciviousness, and dirty language are just so much graffiti written on the bathroom wall for all the effect they have in exorcising the code of respectability his Jewish parents have instilled within him. Consequently, at the age of thirty-three, Portnoy is not only imprisoned by a superego that sounds like the voice of his mother, he is also debilitated by an overwhelming sense of guilt. Describing himself as a Freudian case study, he offers up his repressions, inhibitions, and complexes to the scrutiny of Dr. Spielvogel, his psychoanalyst, in a diatribe that is sheer exhibitionism.

This diatribe, couched as a confession, constitutes the novel. *Portnoy's Complaint* is told in narrative blocks arranged around the protagonist's confessions and only loosely linear in chronology. Student of Freud that he is, Portnoy takes himself back to his earliest childhood memories to begin his account of the forces that turned him into a tormented fugitive from family and culture. Consequently, the book and his recollections begin with a description of his mother: "the most unforgettable character I've met."

Sophie Portnoy is portrayed as sexual, intriguing, and powerful in an almost magical way. She is the object of Alex's first sexual impulses, a fact that he readily acknowledges and that is obviously intended to summon up the conditions of Freud's Oedipus complex.[14] Alex describes her as being so "deeply embedded" in his consciousness that he mistakes his teachers for her when he begins school and later attempts to rape an Israeli woman who, he realizes in analysis, closely resembles his mother. She is not only the central figure in his infantile fantasies and adult sexual aggressions, she is also the arbiter of goodness and morality in the household—the commanding Jewish mother under whose tutelage Portnoy learns the lessons of "self-control, sobriety, and sanctions." Thus, Portnoy presents Sophie as the object of his oedipal fixation and the stereotypic Jewish mother combined to explain the irrevocable influence she has over his life.

The father in this Freudian allegory with overtones of a Jewish folktale also fits two roles. As the third component in an oedipal situation, he is the object of Alex's jealousy and rage. Portnoy remembers a scene when, as a young child, he basked in his mother's undivided attention and wished that the man they called his father would never return from work. He also recalls a period of rage when he wanted to commit violence upon his father's "ignorant, barbaric carcass." Yet as the father in this Jewish family, Jake (or Jack) Portnoy is actually rather ineffectual and poses no real threat to Alex's love-hate relationship with Sophie. He is the typical hardworking family man who dreams of his son's having opportunities that were denied to him. Portnoy admits that "in that ferocious and self-annihilating way to which so many Jewish men of his generation served their families, my father served my mother, my sister Hannah, but particularly me. Where he had been imprisoned, I would fly: that was his dream." Portnoy, however, experiences Jake's love and sacrifice for him as a burden that contributes to his guilt and keeps him ambivalent about his father. Unable to separate and simplify his emotions for the man whose inadequacies can move him both to tears and to rage, Portnoy asks Dr. Spielvogel a most provocative question about human relationships: "Doctor, what should I rid myself of, tell me, the hatred . . . or the love?"

This ambivalence about his parents, the conditions which produced it, and the consequences of it constitute the subject of the novel. After establishing the centrality of his mother to his earliest childhood memories, Alex moves back and forth in his monologue between reminiscences of his childhood and family life and recollections of his sexual urges and frustrations from adolescence to "manhood." From first to last chapter, however, the unifying element among all these disparate memories is Portnoy's consciousness of himself in conflict—with his parents, with his Jewishness, and with his desire to live autonomously and guilt-free. He is caught in what is perhaps the most complex and effective double bind to be depicted in literature.

Portnoy describes his predicament quite simply as one of being "torn by desires that are repugnant to my conscience, and a conscience repugnant to my desires." His conscience requires that he respond to his parents' guidance and love by being a "nice little Jewish boy"—dutiful, respectable, and continent. His desire to be a "man," the self-determining investigator of his passions and appetites, urges him to break whatever parental and cultural taboos restrict his individuality. To be "good" with conviction is to remain a boy; to be "bad" with abandon is to become a man. The double bind for Portnoy is that he can neither be good without feeling diminished nor be bad without feeling guilty. He attempts to resolve the dilemma by asserting his autonomy in secret, through expressions of sexuality, while maintaining the appearance of conformity to his parents' notion of goodness; but that only intensifies his guilt and shame. His desire, as he tells his mother in one of his imaginary retorts, is "to be bad—and enjoy it!" But since he finds that impossible to achieve by his own will, he pleads with Dr. Spielvogel: "Bless me with manhood! Make me brave! Make me strong! Make me *whole!* Enough being a nice Jewish boy, publicly pleasing my parents while privately pulling my putz! Enough!"

Against the suffocating ubiquity of his mother, Portnoy pits his penis, which he describes symbolically as his "battering ram to freedom." As an adolescent, masturbation becomes his primary method of self-assertion, and the voice of the imaginary being who rouses his appetites and calls him "Big Boy" momentarily drowns out the monitory tones of his mother. Finally, when he is thirty-two, this fantasy woman who had urged him to solitary sexual excess materializes as a flesh-and-blood sexual enthusiast whom he calls "The Monkey." She becomes Portnoy's partner in erotic experimentation, fulfilling his adolescent dreams; but the more he enjoys her, the more he lives in fear of public exposure and of jeopardizing his position as Assistant Commissioner of Human Opportunity for the City of New York.

Portnoy feels guilty about the disparity between his public role as a humanitarian and his private pleasure in what he views as degradation, just as in his adolescence he had felt guilty about the disjunction between his public image as a nice Jewish boy and his private profligacy. Consequently, he discovers that sex with women, like masturbation, leaves him confused. He thumbs his nose at the sanctions in order to assert his independence of them, only to find that he is overcome with guilt and fear—the sanctions undo him every time. Far from helping Portnoy batter his way to freedom, his penis, as the symbol of his defiance and his obsession with self, alienates him from the sustaining aspects of family and culture and imprisons him within his own conscience. The poignancy of this condition emerges in his question: "How have I come to be such an enemy and flayer of myself? And so alone! Oh, so alone! Nothing but *self!* Locked up in *me!*" Rather than liberating him, Portnoy's sexual exploits condemn him to solitary confinement within a guilt-ridden self. As Roth adroitly puts it in one of his interviews, "the joke on Portnoy is that for him breaking the taboo turns out to be as unmanning in the end as honoring it."

It is one of the primary ironies of this novel, so renowned for its unrestrained treatment of sex, that it actually undercuts the efficacy of sexuality as a sacred rite of passage to manhood and freedom. For all his maneuvering to satisfy his lusts and exorcise his mother in the process, Portnoy is still locked up in his childish fear of retribution. For all his bravado, he continues to imagine himself as a little boy threatened by his mother with a knife because he will not eat. The sophisticated analysand, he translates this scene of Sophie wielding the bread knife into a "threat of castration" that restrains his sexual freedom and coerces him into a semblance of conformity. Consequently, no amount of sexual activity convinces him that he is truly a man, independent of his mother's direction.

Portnoy does, however, remember two nonsexual experiences that produced a sense of wholeness and freedom. One occurs when he plays center field for a softball team, and the other when he goes with his father to the Turkish baths. Both center field and the baths offer sanctuary from his mother. Portnoy de-

scribes being in center field in terms of glorious alone-
ness in space and of perspective—as a position in
which "you are able to see everything and everyone, to understand what's happening the instant it
happens." The clarity of vision he achieves here is in
sharp contrast to the confusing view of things he has
at home, where his mother alternately smothers him
with love and disregards his vulnerability. And he
feels at ease playing baseball, having mastered all
the moves to the point where he responds instinc-
tively with the right motion, the right gesture. Reflecting on this feeling of assurance that for him was
limited to the baseball field, Portnoy realizes that
"there are people who feel in life the ease, the self-
assurance, the simple and essential affiliation with
what is going on, that I used to feel as the center
fielder for the Seabees."

Similarly, Portnoy experiences this "simple and essential affiliation" on his monthly visits with his father
to the baths. In fact, in recalling this regular retreat
from everyday aggravations, Portnoy describes being
in the company only of men as the most basic and
primitive kind of affiliation. The masculine world of
the steam room reminds him of prehistoric times, of
"some sloppy watery time, before there were families
such as we know them." The implication is that men
without the civilizing influence of women can prof-
itably revert to primitivism. Certainly Portnoy indicates that in association with these Jewish men he
changes for the better, ceasing for a while to be the
nice little boy in quest of his mother's approbation. He
feels safe here, and, most significantly, he thinks of
this habitat that is the exclusive domain of men as
"natural" because it is a place "without *goyim* and
women."

Such an antipathy for, and fear of, Gentiles and
women seems, on the surface, peculiar in a man who

generally rejects his parents' attitudes about Jewishness and is obsessed with sleeping with shikses. Portnoy consistently asserts his humanity over his Jewishness in response to the distinction he sees his family making between things that are Jewish and things that are "goyische." But asserting that he *"happen*[s] *also to be a human being"* does not prevent Portnoy from feeling disenfranchised in a country where a Jew does not fit the media image of an American.

Nurtured on movies and radio programs in which Gentiles typify Americans, Portnoy finds himself caught between his own Jewish culture and the picture of the pervasive American culture he has imbibed from the media. He has learned from the movies that "America is a *shikse* nestling under your arm," and so he yearns for this mysterious "Other" as the fulfillment of the American dream; but his Jewish teachings forbid his having her, and his Jewishness ostracizes him from her. This conflict manifests itself as a defiant obsession with possessing "Thereal McCoy," an idealized version of the all-American girl that arises from both envy and hatred. He envies these gentile girls their "grammatical fathers" and "composed mothers" and their harmonious family life. At the same time, he hates them for being the "real" Americans and for what this authenticity implies about his own cultural legitimacy. As a result of these conflicts and ambivalences, Portnoy's sexual experiences with several gentile girls represent more than the simple gratification of his lust. His sexual acts with the blond, blue-eyed daughters of the dominant culture are a kind of vengeance against the image of the American Dream whose reality is inaccessible to him; they are, as he finally admits, attempts to *"conquer* America."

In recounting his sexual aggression against gentile girls (and their American backgrounds), Portnoy reveals the extent to which women are primarily representational to him. He identifies most of his conquests, for example, by names that describe what they represent to him rather than by their proper names. There is first Kay Campbell, his "girl friend" at Antioch College, who is sensible, midwestern, and Protestant; he calls her "The Pumpkin." Then there is Sarah Abbott Maulsby, an aristocratic New Englander, whom he calls "The Pilgrim." Finally, there is Mary Jane Reed, a semiliterate hillbilly from West Virginia, who seems to love Portnoy and whom he calls "The Monkey." These women are primarily types to Portnoy, characterized first by being non-Jewish and next by being representative of a particular segment of Americana. Their individuality is of no real significance to Portnoy because he seems to be constitutionally incapable of loving women with whom he has a sexual relationship. It is only in fleeting moments with "The Monkey" that he can manage to unite desire and feelings of affection. Most of the time his desire is mixed with feelings of contempt for the women whose gentile "differentness" is both their primary attraction and the thing he despises.

Whatever success he has in subjugating the shikses, Portnoy is never able to assuage his sense of separateness as a Jewish-American. As the book ends, he takes a trip to Israel, partly to escape the intensity of his personal conflicts and partly to try to reach some conclusions about his Jewish-American identity. Ironically, he discovers that in the Jewish homeland he is as much an isolate as he ever was in Newark and that there even his sexuality cannot be relied upon to provide him with a semblance of control over his destiny. All the strands of Portnoy's several conflicts—his guilt over sexuality, his oedipal fixation, his sense of alienation from American culture because of his Jewishness and from the Jewish culture because of his violation of its sanctions—come together here in Portnoy's brief encounter with an Israeli woman named Naomi.

He envisions this freckled, redheaded Jewish girl, who at first reminds him of his midwestern "Pumpkin" and later of his mother, as his salvation. He thinks that she will make him whole, bring together the warring elements of Jewishness and sexuality, mother and shikse. She turns out to be, however, his "final downfall and humiliation." When she rebuffs his advances, he attempts to rape her, only to discover that he is impotent—"Im-po-tent in Is-rael," as Portnoy sings to himself in realizing the symbolic irony of his condition. After his defeat, Portnoy is left whimpering on the floor like a child and still fearful of retribution for not being "good." His obscenity and sexual aggression have not freed him; they have left him full of rage and self-hatred and, ultimately, impotent—powerless. The novel ends with Portney's howl of frustration and the enigmatic words of Dr. Spielvogel: "Now vee may perhaps to begin. Yes?" This is the punch line of the extended joke about guilt and the desire for autonomy that constitutes the novel.

In coming to realize what he calls "guilt . . . as a comic idea" and allowing that realization to dictate the concerns and methods of *Portnoy's Complaint,* Roth acknowledges a new literary influence. *Letting Go* had been full of Jamesian references and, at times, had been suggestive of the Jamesian style. *When She Was Good* had been evocative of Flaubert in its authorial detachment and had recalled specifically *Madame Bovary* [15] in its rendering of bourgeois conventionality and its presentation of a woman who chafes at the restrictions of life and the weaknesses of men. In each of these earlier novels, Roth's tone had been serious and somber. Like Peter Tarnopol, the writer in *My Life as a Man,* Roth had shown himself to be a devotee of "complicated fictions of moral anguish." But in turning to the comic mode for *Portnoy's Complaint,* Roth did not abandon the fiction of moral anguish. He merely shifted his perspective enough to discover that an obsession with moral anguish is potentially comic; and this discovery, Roth suggests, came through the German writer Franz Kafka, one of the most serious of fictionalists.[16] Picturing Kafka "giggling" while he composed his grim stories of conflict and remorse, Roth realized, he says, that "it was all so funny, this morbid preoccupation with punishment and guilt. Hideous, but funny."

In translating this perspective into *Portnoy's Complaint,* Roth was obviously not concerned with writing a "Kafkaesque" novel in the usual sense of that term; but he does take the Kafkaesque preoccupation with victimization and guilt to its limits in an exaggeration that resembles burlesque. He structures a situation that has the optimum possibilities for producing guilt: the "nice Jewish boy," mothered, adored, and protected, in conflict with family and culture as he attempts to exercise the libidinous side of his nature. He endows his protagonist with an acute sense of himself as the guilt-ridden victim of parental conditioning, and he places him on the analyst's couch, where he is free to indulge in excoriating his parents and exploring his psyche. He then turns the narrative over to this protagonist, who regards himself not only as the casualty of an oedipal conflict but also as the "smothered son in the Jewish joke." The result is a novel of excess, where the language is hyperbolic and the style exclamatory, and where guilt, recrimination, and rage are inflated to Gargantuan proportions.

While Roth may have found in Kafka a perspective for the comic mode of *Portnoy's Complaint,* a substantial portion of the material for the novel was embedded in Roth's previous work. This is not meant to suggest that the novel is merely a reworking of previous themes but to emphasize the point that, despite departures in tone and style, Roth's work is consistent in the concerns it addresses. Perhaps more than any other of Roth's novels, *Portnoy's Complaint* is the culmination of a series of fictional efforts—a compendium of themes that, in combination, reach their zenith in this book constructed on exaggeration.

For example, the question that Neil Klugman in *Goodbye, Columbus* asks himself, "But how carnal can I get?" becomes Portnoy's challenge as he attempts through his various sexual exploits to "PUT THE ID BACK IN YID!" Similarly, other questions, conditions, and themes from the earlier fiction emerge in this novel. Neil Klugman's inability to commit himself fully to a love relationship is reflected and expanded in Portnoy's incapacity for commitment to any one of a series of women. The question of what it means to be a Jew in America that dominates "Eli, the Fanatic" also absorbs Portnoy, who would willingly trade his "suffering heritage" for "Thereal Mc-Coy." The association of sexuality with guilt that is played out in the story of adultery in "Epstein," as well as the equation of sexual assertiveness with freedom, becomes central in *Portnoy*. Ozzie Freedman's defiance of the restrictiveness of his religion in "The Conversion of the Jews" anticipates Portnoy's "refusal to be bound any longer by taboos which . . . *he* experiences as diminishing and unmanning"; in fact, Roth acknowledges that Alexander Portnoy is an "older incarnation of claustrophobic little Freedman." However, Roth suggests, Portnoy is less oppressed by external forces than Ozzie and more the victim of his own rage than anything else, and in this he is an appropriate counterpart to Lucy Nelson, the defiant heroine of *When She Was Good*. Finally, the potential for the characterization of the ubiquitous mother and the long-suffering father whose influence is pervasive in *Portnoy* can be found in *Letting Go*. Portnoy's constipated and passive father is, in many ways, a blend of Gabe Wallach's and Paul Herz's fathers; and Sophie Portnoy, the most vivid of Jewish mothers, dominant and omnipresent in her son's consciousness, appears to be a fleshed-out version of Gabe Wallach's mother. Each of them exerts a powerful influence on her son's behavior; each thinks of herself as being, perhaps, a little "too good." Yet if Anna Wallach prefigures Sophie Portnoy in many ways, it is still Sophie one thinks of as the archetypal Jewish mother; and this fuller realization of her character reflects largely the extent of Alex's obsession with her. She is presented exclusively through his perspective, yet so indelibly etched is she in his memory that she comes to life in a way that Anna Wallach was never intended to do.

Although *Portnoy's Complaint* is a climactic novel for Roth in the sense that several of his previous themes reach their greatest intensity of expression here, the originality of the mode of the novel attracted new and unprecedented attention to Roth's work. The confessional aspect of the book coincided with a current in the 1960s that was tolerant of candor, and Portnoy's impious baring of the psyche to reveal his obsessions and secret degradations made his creator famous—and also notorious. For not all the reactions to *Portnoy's Complaint* were favorable. Many readers found the indecorous language offensive, and segments of the Jewish community were incensed at what they determined to be its anti-Semitic overtones. The extent to which the novel was regarded at once as a success and a scandal is indicated by the dual reviews the *Saturday Review* carried when *Portnoy* first appeared. One review called it "something very much like a masterpiece" [17]; the other called it a "mixture of bile, sperm, and self-indulgence." [18] Long after *Portnoy* had become a bestseller, this duality of response continued. Some readers questioned the novel's artistic merit, and others maintained that it was a masterful demonstration of the confusion that afflicts not only Portnoy but many of us in one way or another.

Roth himself has been quite prolific in attempting to explain why the obscenity that many regarded as gratuitous is actually integral to the novel. He has also acknowledged the irony that it was his most controversial book which brought him fame. In a particularly poignant essay, he indicates that his training had instilled within him a sense of the "moral seriousness" of art and of the priestly vocation of the artist. He assumed, then, that if fame ever came to him, it would come as it had to Aschenbach, the artist in Thomas Mann's *Death in Venice,* as "Honor." Aschenbach, of course, had wrought his art out of Apollonian restraint and gave vent only in his personal fantasies to the Dionysian side of his nature.[19] Ironically, Roth, the author of several restrained and morally serious works, achieved fame through the artistic expression of the Dionysian side of Portnoy's nature and found himself personally identified with "everything that Aschenbach had suppressed and kept a shameful secret right down to his morally resolute end."

In addition to being the novel that catapulted Roth into the public view, *Portnoy's Complaint* represents something of a turning point in Roth's work. Beginning with *Goodbye, Columbus,* the issue of personal sovereignty versus external authority had been presented in various ways, but its most pervasive expression up through *Portnoy* had been in terms of the individual in conflict with the family. This family conflict becomes more central with each succeeding novel and gains in intensity from one novel to another until it reaches a peak in *Portnoy's Complaint*. Roth's exploration, for example, of the individual's experience of the family as a conditioning and controlling force figures significantly but somewhat indirectly in *Letting Go*, dominates *When She Was Good*, and becomes the *raison d'être* for *Portnoy's Complaint*. Alexander Portnoy is Roth's most vocal exemplar of resistance to the authority of the family and the most self-conscious and intentional "bad boy" among his characters.

After *Portnoy's Complaint*, however, Roth seems less engrossed with the family as the central force in his characters' lives. Although the family conflict still has a place in *The Professor of Desire, My Life as a Man,* and *The Ghost Writer,* in these later works the family as determinant is subordinate to characterological determinism—those aspects of the protagonist's nature which he struggles to reconcile or overcome. Subsequent to *Portnoy,* Roth's characters are divested of the adolescent rage against their parents that distinguishes Alex and his female counterpart, Lucy Nelson. Seemingly, while Portnoy's attempts to dispossess himself of his family's dominance failed, Roth's exorcism of his own preoccupation with the family worked, and the writing of the novel allowed him to turn toward investigating other manifestations of the problem of self-determination.

2

ooooooooooooooooooooooooooooooooooooooooooooo

A Rake among Scholars,
A Scholar among Rakes

Early in his journey from blissful childhood to confused, disillusioned, and impotent manhood, David
Kepesh (*The Professor of Desire*) discovers that his
intellectuality and his sexuality are at odds. He realizes that, like Byron,[1] he wants to be "studious by
day, dissolute by night" and, like Richard Steele,[2]
fancies himself "a rake among scholars, a scholar
among rakes." For a time, these prototypes offer him a
"bit of prestigious justification for [his] high grades
and [his] base desires"; but throughout his life he
fights a recurring battle between passion and reason,
pleasure and duty, violent self-assertion and dedication to the discipline of his profession as a teacher and
scholar.

This conflict between high-minded moral responsibility and sensuous self-assertion is central to the
plight of the Roth hero. Neil Klugman experiences it
as an unresolvable tension between his affectional instincts and his carnal and acquisitive tendencies, and
Portnoy knows it as outright war between his humanitarian impulses and his determined lustfulness. Roth
often represents this conflict through the life of a college professor (*Letting Go, The Breast, The Professor of Desire, My Life as a Man*) or a member of some
other profession associated with service to humankind
(*Goodbye, Columbus, Portnoy's Complaint*). In this

way he connects the Apollonian sense of order and moderation with the ideals of the protagonist's profession, and associates the Dionysian compulsion for unconventionality and excess with the protagonist's private life.

Although the scholar-rake metaphor that expresses this Apollonian-Dionysian conflict is clearest in Roth's later books, it has its seeds in the early fiction. In *Goodbye, Columbus,* the disjunctiveness of Neil Klugman's public and private lives, although less extreme than for later protagonists, foreshadows the familiar struggle. Neil is, temporarily at least, practicing one of those intellectual careers typical of the Roth hero, and it is at his job in the Newark library that he is his most compassionate and humane. There, he identifies with and becomes involved in attempting to protect a black child who comes to the library to escape the hardships of ghetto life. But, off duty, he is caught up in a love-hate relationship with Brenda Patimkin and her upwardly mobile, Americanized family. This involvement grows out of what he calls the "acquisitiveness" in himself—his desire for sexual expression, his attraction to the advantages that money can buy. Like other Roth characters, he cannot seem to balance the dualities of his nature: a side that responds to the ideals and moral imperatives associated with a humane or literary vocation and a side that seeks unrestrained self-gratification. It is significant that as his relationship with Brenda intensifies, Neil takes a vacation from the library to spend all his time with her; when the affair is over, it is to the library that he returns. Because the job and the love affair seem to draw upon antithetical aspects of his nature, they are largely unintegrated experiences for Neil, just as his conflicting desires are unintegrated. This is a variant of the conflict dramatized repeatedly by Roth but never fully resolved.

Neil Klugman predicts the later "professors of desire" in that, like all of them, he is a college graduate with a humanities degree, and his job suggests his commitment to the "humane" and the literary. But it is in *Letting Go* that Roth first begins to make the literature professor the battleground for the internal war between self-control and self-assertion. Both Gabe Wallach and Paul Herz, the two professors of the novel, are remote, fastidious academicians who are fearful of emotional entanglements. Unlike Kepesh and Portnoy, they are prone to be cautious rather than impetuous; and they each exemplify in different degrees the humanitarian-professor who prefers the ordered life to the complexities of human involvement and experience. But Gabe, because he has a greater need for proving himself than Paul, is more of a risk taker and closer to the typically divided scholar of the later books. He at least recognizes the limitations and dangerous repressions of the "safe," responsible, scholarly life. Paul, however, in deciding that he is a man of duty rather than feeling, abandons the struggle with conflicting desires and in his rejection of the encounter brings upon himself a psychic disaster that is almost total. His self-sacrificing, restraining, religious impulses come to dominate him almost to the point of autism; by the end of the book, he has cut himself off from all of those adventurous, albeit troublesome, urges which plague the other professors and yet connect them to the rest of humanity. In one of the last scenes of the book, Paul's wife accuses him of giving up, and he responds, "I've perhaps given in."

Paul Herz is Roth's only major male character who totally refuses to combat the conflict between duty and feeling, restraint and assertion, and who, in refusing the battle, inadvertently chooses restraint. As the example of Gabe Wallach suggests and that of

David Kepesh in *The Professor of Desire* makes clear, it is the conflict itself that gives vitality to the typical Roth protagonist. Sometimes the rake overcomes the scholar, and sometimes it is the other way around; but both the rake and the scholar are necessary aspects of the protagonist's nature. Without the rake's urging him to adventure, to sensuous self-expression, the scholar becomes withdrawn—a dutiful automaton; and without the scholar's cracking the whip of conscience, the rake becomes a pathological libertine. Either condition becomes a kind of stasis.

Although the characteristic Roth protagonist—torn between body and soul, extroversion and introversion—is prefigured in Neil Klugman, Paul Herz, and Gabe Wallach, it is not until *Portnoy's Complaint* that the type becomes distinct. The "complaint" that structures the book is itself a statement of the Roth hero's pervasive conflict. Dr. Spielvogel defines Portnoy's complaint as a "disorder in which strongly-felt ethical and altruistic impulses are perpetually warring with extreme sexual longings, often of a perverse nature" and suggests that Portnoy's "morality" inhibits sexual gratification and produces shame and fear. He locates the source of the disorder in the "mother-child relationship," a diagnosis that is much more crucial for this novel's meaning and structure than for any of Roth's others. The first half of the book concentrates on the family that produced Portnoy and his complaint and establishes Sophie Portnoy as the powerful prohibitor of her son's appetites—for junk food, sex, and everything non-Jewish. Consequently, Portnoy, who is torn between wanting to be a good Jewish boy and a sexual acrobat, has a more obvious object against which to vent his rage than later protagonists, who also experience the conflict between ethical impulses and sexual desires. Here the conflict is at least partially external—Portnoy versus his family; in later novels it becomes increasingly internalized, the story of a man at war with himself.

Although he is not a writer and college teacher like David Kepesh or Peter Tarnopol, Portnoy is actually the first of Roth's scholar-rakes, in the extended meaning of that metaphor. His ethical and altruistic bent is reflected in the position he holds as Assistant Commissioner of Human Opportunity, just as Kepesh's and Tarnopol's similar inclinations are indicated by their attachments to the literary vocations of teaching and writing. And, like them, Portnoy finds incongruous his public life as a member of a respectable profession based on moral principles and his private life of profligacy.

Throughout his involvement with the uninhibited and uneducated woman whom he calls "The Monkey," Portnoy worries about the disjunction between his "position" and his sex life; and while the rake in him cannot believe his good fortune in having such a beautiful and acquiescent sexual partner, the scholar sees it as inappropriate and fears retribution. At one point, Portnoy thinks: "This is the kind of girl ordinarily seen hanging from the arm of a Mafiosa or a movie star, not the 1950 valedictorian of Weequahic High! Not the editor of the *Columbia Law Review*! Not the highminded civil-libertarian!" For Portnoy, the conflict between high ideals and base desires is irreconcilable. Tutored in "goodness" by his family, he cannot believe that he can have it both ways—do good for mankind and still enjoy a "fifty-foot fashion model."

The emergence of the scholar-rake as a "pure" type in Roth's fiction is an evolutionary process. *Goodbye, Columbus* and *Letting Go* adumbrate his inclination for a career associated with the humane and the literary. *Portnoy's Complaint* defines his conflict and depicts its psychological origins. And, finally, *The*

Breast, My Life as a Man, and *The Professor of Desire* work as a kind of trilogy that rounds out the character. The scholar-rake becomes fully developed as the "professor of desire" in the last of these three novels and there momentarily transcends the professor-desire dichotomy. Through the struggles of young Nathan Zuckerman, the protagonist of Roth's latest published fictional piece, *The Ghost Writer,* the conflict between restraint and license, reserve and flamboyance, which had previously been played out largely in terms of a purely personal dilemma, becomes an artistic problem as well.

The Breast

From the first in Roth's fiction, his characters have labored to come to terms with themselves as they act in ways uncharacteristic of their own self-images and attempt to reconcile the dualities within themselves. But previous to *The Breast,* they were precipitated into self-examination and self-definition largely by their own extreme reactions to rather familiar circumstances, such as the pressures of their families or their cultural environments. In *The Breast,* Roth structures an extreme situation over which his protagonist, David Kepesh, has no control, and renders the struggle for self-definition unavoidable by making Kepesh's alien self physical rather than psychological.

Inexplicably, Kepesh, a fairly stable and "civilized" young literature professor, is transformed into a one-hundred-fifty-five-pound human breast. No amount of searching into family origins or social conditions explains the cause of his metamorphosis; and although Kepesh himself (and perhaps the reader) would like to interpret his problem as psychological rather than physical, the fact that he has actually turned into a breast is what Kepesh must accept and what the reader must not, at least, disallow. By having Kepesh narrate his own story, Roth makes the question of the reality of this bizarre situation the primary issue of the book and causes the reader to participate in the protagonist's attempt to find a plausible explanation for an incredible event. Kepesh finally learns, however, that neither psychology nor literature, the two "healing" arts with which he is most familiar, can explain away the fact that he experiences life as a blind, exquisitely tactile mound of spherical flesh.

Before the transformation narrows his life to the single issue of anatomy, Kepesh has managed to survive a tempestuous marriage and divorce and to gain a fair measure of equilibrium. He has done so primarily by drawing upon his own reserves of dignity and decorum and by electing to forgo relationships with women of "spontaneity and temperament" for a relationship with an "even-tempered and predictable" fourth-grade teacher, Claire Ovington. Theirs is a sensible and orderly relationship—a little short on passion, perhaps—but Kepesh persuades himself that he has reached that stage in his life "where the calm harbor and its clear, placid waters" is preferable to the "foaming drama of the high seas." He has subdued the rake in himself and is relying on the qualities that characterize the scholar, or professor. These qualities he enumerates later as he tells his psychoanalyst, Dr. Klinger: "I was never 'strong.' Only determined. One foot in front of the other. Punctuality. Honesty. Courtesy. Good grades in all subjects. It goes back to my handing my homework in on time and carrying off the prizes."

Just when Kepesh is feeling "grounded, dug in," and stable, his ordered life erupts. He turns overnight into what Theodore Solotaroff calls the "grotesque image of his deepest fear (and desire)." [3] The details of the metamorphosis itself are vague—first, because Kepesh, the narrator, remembers practically nothing about the hours during which he mysteriously changed from a man into a breast, and second, because Roth concentrates more on showing Kepesh's reactions to his new form than on delineating how it came into being. The focus of the book is on what Roth calls Kepesh's "unrelenting education in his own misfortune." Repeatedly, and against his will, he is forced to confront the reality of a physical identity that is foreign to him. Yet inside all the adipose tissue that constitutes his new physical self, Kepesh is mentally alive as his old self; and the story that he narrates is of his attempts to assert mind over matter— to use the stock of mental equipment that he had as a man to challenge and explain away his condition as a breast. "Either I continue to be myself, or I will go mad," he proclaims shortly after the disaster has occurred; but no effort of will can reconcile the disparity between his mental self-image and the appearance he presents to the world.

In a succession of stages, which he chronicles as "crises," the protagonist-narrator begins his education in experiencing life as a mammary gland. The first major crisis occurs when he discovers the erotic qualities of his "body." He goes into a sexual frenzy every time he is touched and soon becomes consumed with sexual cravings that he wants Claire to fulfill. She accommodates him to some degree, but she can never satisfy his fantasies completely because Kepesh fears both to divulge to her the extent of his lustful longings and to indulge himself in them. The professor is busy keeping the rake in check and persuading him that if he acts upon his "base" and "disgusting" sexual urges, he will lose all claim to love, happiness, and sanity. Kepesh thinks he will drive Claire away if he asks her to perform the bizarre acts he craves, and,

like Portnoy, he is always afraid that his sexual per-
version is about to be exposed (he is convinced that
his every move is being televised or tape-recorded).
Most important, he refrains from asking Claire to provide him with complete gratification because he
fears that indulgence will accustom him to grotesqueries and, ultimately, drive him mad. Arguing that
his restraint stems from self-preservation rather than
conscience, he says:

What alarmed me so about giving in to this grotesque
yearning was that by so doing I might be severing myself
irreparably from my own past and my own kind. I was
afraid that if I were to become habituated to such practices, my appetites could only become progressively
strange, until at last I reached a peak of disorientation
from which I would fall—or leap—into the void. I would
go mad. I would cease to know who I had been or what
I was.

Kepesh survives this initial crisis in his existence
as a totally erogenous being by opting for control and
moderation. He subdues his fantasies until they are
almost completely manageable, and he allots himself
a half hour of stimulation during Claire's hour-long
visits. Even in his extreme condition, he requires himself to be sensible about his sexuality for fear that he
will become even more disconnected than he is from
his "own past" and his "own kind."

Kepesh's second major crisis in coping with his
transformation involves what he calls his "crisis of
faith." He refuses to believe that he is a breast and
takes refuge in thinking that he is mad. While the
rake had been most in evidence during Kepesh's sexual phase of reaction (only to be subdued by the reasonable professor), the professor is clearly dominant
during this second, mental phase. As a literature
teacher familiar with the great stories of transforma-

tion as told by Swift, Gogol, and Kafka,[4] Kepesh
latches onto these literary prototypes to explain the
cause of what he wants to believe is a delusion. Giving full credence to the idea that imaginative literature can alter one's way of perceiving reality, he at
first suggests that his involvement in the stories he
had been teaching brought about his delusion of being
a breast. "I got it from fiction," he tells Dr. Klinger.

Later, as Kepesh begins to entertain the idea that
he is not mad after all, he still attributes to literature
the power to influence his actual transformation. He
theorizes that he fell so completely under the sway
of the "great imaginations" who created fictions of
transformation that he attempted to bridge the gap
between art and life and to make the fictions real by
actually undergoing a metamorphosis. He believes that
he has taken the leap beyond sublimation and turned
the imaginary into the real, thereby surpassing
even Swift, Gogol, and Kafka. As he tells Dr. Klinger:
"I made the word flesh. I have out-Kafkaed Kafka.
He could only *imagine* a man turning into a cock-
roach. But look what I have done!"

Although initially literature serves Kepesh in his
attempts to escape the reality of his predicament, it
finally is the means by which he comes to accept the
fact of his altered physical existence. On the level on
which *The Breast* implies a perspective about the relationship of literature and life, it suggests that art is
both a way of escaping everyday reality and of con-
fronting it. By believing that he has "made the
word flesh," Kepesh is at last able to confront reality
and to accept that he is a breast; but this happens
only because the word is there to make the flesh comprehensible. Literature clarifies life for this protagonist, as Kepesh's acceptance of his condition indicates
and as the conclusion of the book reiterates. Kepesh,
teacher to the last, ends his narrative with a lecture

and a poem. The lecture reaches its climax with the declaration, "I am David Alan Kepesh, the Breast, and I will live by my own lights." The poem, "Archaic Torso of Apollo," by the German poet Rainer Maria Rilke, concludes with the recognition and the admonition that

> . . . there is no place
> that does not see you. You must
>   change your life.

Taken together, Kepesh's declaration of selfhood and the words of the Rilke poem indicate that the protagonist is beginning to realize the equal pitfalls of attempting to whip his rakish nature into conformity and of allowing it license only in secret. Yet it is the voice of the professor speaking, and the professorial side must not be discarded either. If Kepesh takes to heart the Rilke imperative, "You must / change your life," he will realize that ultimately his identity is determined by his behavior—a truth he is just beginning to learn. Circumstances have already changed Kepesh externally; it is up to him to change internally, to harmonize the professor and the rake.

Roth has said that "perhaps the man who turns into a breast is the first heroic character I've ever been able to portray." Certainly he is the first Roth protagonist to glimpse that he alone has primary responsibility for his behavior and to realize the close connection between behavior and identity. He is also the first in a series of academicians in Roth's fiction who find in literature a viable means of objectifying personal reality. It remains for Peter Tarnopol in *My Life as a Man* and Kepesh, who recurs as the protagonist in *The Professor of Desire*, to show more fully the ways in which literature can facilitate the transformation of the professor-rake into what may be called the "conscientious professor"—a man who finds in his

literary vocation a way to integrate the best qualities
of each half of his dichotomous nature.

More a mode of perception and a quality of existence than anything else, the conscientious professor,
when he emerges, represents the most mature aspects of the Roth protagonist. He has dispossessed
himself, at least momentarily, of the need to be a
good boy merely for the sake of his parents and has
accepted his need to achieve, to be disciplined, and
to be humane as the dictates of his own nature. He
also recognizes the positive values and the energizing
potential of self-assertion. And although he is never
able to maintain this state of wholeness permanently,
when he does achieve it, it is because he has found
in the word—in literature—a way to integrate the
spirit and the flesh. He discovers that in teaching
literature, he teaches life; and he finds in artistic invention a way of making some sense of his own experiential reality.

My Life as a Man

More than anything else, *My Life as a Man* is about
the attempt to describe and define experiential reality
through literature—through teaching it and especially
through creating it. In its structure and its major concern, the novel exhibits Roth's fascination with the relationship between fiction and fact and his interest in
the use a writer makes of his personal experiences in
the creative process. Here he sets up a complex
structure in which a writer creates a piece of fiction
about a writer (a thinly veiled version of himself) and
then discusses in his own voice the importance of
the self to the novelist. The double irony is, of course,
that behind the artist creating a fictionalized writer is
Philip Roth creating the artist, whose biographical de-

tails clearly resemble his own. It is as if in construct-
ing these layers of perspective Roth set out to accomplish what Philip Quarles, one of the characters in
Aldous Huxley's novel *Point Counter Point*, proposes as
a novelistic scheme:

Put a novelist in the novel. He justifies aesthetic general-
izations. . . . He also justifies experiment. Specimens of
his work may illustrate other possible or impossible ways
of telling a story. . . . But why draw the line at one novelist inside your novel? Why not a second inside his? And
a third inside the novel of the second? And so on to infinity
like those advertisements of Quaker Oats where there's a
Quaker holding a box of oats, on which is a picture of another Quaker holding another box of oats, on which etc., etc.[5]

Instead of expressing these multiple dimensions of fiction as a succession of pictures on a Quaker Oats box,
Roth chooses to express them as a series of mirrors,
thereby emphasizing the nature of fiction as a re-
fracted reality and the artist's difficulty in achieving
true self-definition through his art.

Roth establishes Peter Tarnopol as the novelist-
professor in this book and has him tell the story of
his life in layers of fiction. Each account of his life
represents Tarnopol's attempt to understand himself
and his experiences by objectifying it all in words. He
first offers "fictionalized" versions of himself in two
short stories, "Salad Days" and "Courting Disaster,"
both of which are labeled "useful fictions." As Tarnopol indicates in the last portion of the book, they are
useful fictions because they serve him in his efforts to
"demystify" and exorcise the past.

In "Salad Days," Tarnopol assumes the stance of
an omniscient narrator to relate the adventures of
young Nathan Zuckerman—his love affair with literature and with his sexual disciple, Sharon Shatzky. In
"Courting Disaster," he shifts to first-person narration,

retaining Zuckerman as the protagonist but altering
the details that describe his background. Finally, ostensibly dispensing with fiction altogether, he presents a long version of his life in an autobiographical
narrative that he calls "My True Story." Here he speaks
in his own voice about the "real" events that underlie
his fiction and wrestles with his inability to achieve
through his writing either a complete exorcism of the
painful parts of his past or a satisfactory definition of
himself. He begins to doubt whether words "born
either of imagination or forthrightness" can ever do
more than approximate the reality they represent. The
problem of how to present himself—in the final
analysis, of how to define himself so that he is comprehensible to himself—is never solved. As Roth says
when he indicates that the subject of *My Life as a
Man* is a process of self-definition involving delicate
distinctions between "real" life and "fictionalized"
life:

But for Tarnopol the presentation or description of himself
is what is most problematical—and what remains unre-
solved. To my mind, Tarnopol's attempt to realize himself
with the right words—as earlier in life he attempted
realizing himself through the right deeds—is what's at the
heart of the book, and accounts for my joining his fictions
about his life with his autobiography. When the novel is
considered in its entirety, I hope it will be understood as
Tarnopol's struggle to achieve a description.

Part of the impetus for Tarnopol's attempt to "realize himself with the right words" stems from his belief
in literature as a device for imposing order upon the
chaotic; and, like all of Roth's scholar-rakes, Tarnopol's
life is a confusion of conflicting desires and allegiances.
He is another of Roth's "nice civilized Jewish" boys
wanting to be a man; yet, like Gabe Wallach, he fears
the "savagery" inherent in "grown-up" relationships

with women. He is attracted to the kind of woman that Roth calls a "knocked-around, on-her-own, volatile, combative, handful" because she provides an authentic test of his manhood; yet when he becomes involved with this type in Maureen Johnson, he is demoralized and emasculated. He is dedicated to "Art of the serious moral variety" and wants, like his literary model Flaubert, to "sow his oats with dusky dancing girls."

All these conflicts begin for Tarnopol when, at twenty-five, he decides to reverse the meaning of the Flaubertian maxim, "Be regular and orderly in your life like a bourgeois, so that you may be violent and original in your work." Concluding that he would prefer a little originality, if not violence, in his life, he decides to tackle a relationship with Maureen, an unpredictable woman with a "daredevil background." This relationship provides him with more violence than he had hoped for, as well as the material for his fiction and the obsession for his autobiography. The "disaster" of his marriage to Maureen sobers the lighthearted tone of "Salad Days" in its concluding pages and is the fictionalized subject of "Courting Disaster." Finally, it is rendered as a "true" account in "My True Story," in which Tarnopol divulges not only the details of his embattled relationship with Maureen but also the extent of his own internal battle between the demands of the rake for originality and energy in his life and those of the professor for regularity and order.

In "Salad Days," Tarnopol narrates the pleasures of Nathan Zuckerman's promising and zestful youth from what he calls an "amused, Olympian point of view." The tale of this innocent stage of Zuckerman's life reads much like some of the early sections of *Portnoy's Complaint* with the addition of a bemused narrator who makes ironic comments about the pro-

tagonist and his behavior. Like Portnoy, Zuckerman is
the protected and self-important child of doting parents who goes through the phase of falling in love
with his mother and frustrates his father with his
arrogance. He is relatively free of Portnoy's guilt,
however, and declares his emotional and intellectual
independence from his family when he goes off to college in Vermont and falls under the spell of literature.
There he imbibes from his mentor, Caroline Benson, a
religious respect for literature and becomes a votary of
Virginia Woolf, Flaubert, and Henry James [6]—novelists of "high seriousness."

Devoted as he is to the "refinement of spirit"
that he identifies with these literary masters and that
he would like to emulate in his own life, the rake demands his satisfactions—and gets them—through the
antics of the rather mindless Sharon Shatzky. Like
"The Monkey," Portnoy's sexual partner, Sharon is
willing to play endless variations upon a sexual theme.
There is, however, from the beginning a flaw in their
sexual arrangement, since the budding professor responds with distaste to the coarseness and ignorance of the rake's sexual playmate. When Sharon
sends him pornographic letters, her redundant style
and errors in punctuation and grammar offend her
lover's sensibilities. Nathan, the literary critic, observes that "instead of acting upon him as an aphro-
disiac, her style frequently jarred him by its banal
insistence." He finally concludes that although Sharon
is a "tantalizing slave," she is "hardly a soul mate" for
someone with his commitment to literature.

In concluding the story, Tarnopol elects to leave
Nathan's relative good fortune and idealism intact.
Drafted upon graduation from college, Zuckerman
had gone through basic training and MP school
dreading the day when he would be sent to Korea; but
an administrative error has caused him to be assigned

instead to Fort Campbell, Kentucky. As the narrator, Tarnopol, indicates, however, this reprieve may be Nathan's last for some time; and in the final paragraphs of the story, he sounds the portent of calamities to come. He predicts that despite the felicity of childhood and young manhood, Zuckerman will know pain "in the form of estrangement, mortification, fierce and unremitting opposition" and that this pain will enter his life "not entirely without invitation." This suggestion that Zuckerman will choose the things that cause him pain precludes the idea that his fate is determined by forces outside himself. In fact, the narrator makes it clear that it is the contradictions in his own nature that will bring him suffering:

He would begin to pay . . . for the vanity and the ignorance, to be sure, but above all for the contradictions; the stinging tongue and the tender hide, the spiritual aspirations and the lewd desires, the soft boyish needs and the manly, the *magisterial* ambitions.

Thus Zuckerman will lose his innocence, not because of external circumstances or ordinary mistakes but because the tender hide, boyish needs, and spiritual aspirations of the professor are at war with the stinging tongue, lewd desires, and magisterial ambitions of the rake.

Suggesting that the narration of Zuckerman's later misfortunes requires a "darker sense of irony" than was appropriate for "Salad Days," Tarnopol turns the telling of the story over to his protagonist in "Courting Disaster." But Tarnopol working through the persona of Zuckerman sounds remarkably like Roth working through the persona of Gabe Wallach in *Letting Go*. The tone of both pieces is sober in contrast to others of the author's stories, and their settings are the same—Chicago's Hyde Park neighborhood and the University of Chicago. The professorial

seriousness and pomposity of the two protagonists are
also the same. Zuckerman, now an English instructor
and a developing writer, is the epitome of scholarly
regularity and order. He maintains a strict regimen of
work outside the classroom, and in his role as teacher
he is "alert to every fine point of conduct," judging
himself by the "strictest standard in every detail." He
also sees himself as superior to almost everyone, including his sister in the suburbs and all the other be-
nighted souls who are not reading "Allen Tate on the
sublime and Dr. Leavis on Matthew Arnold" with
their breakfast cereal.

Like other Roth professors, Zuckerman is particularly attached to this image of himself as a successful literary connoisseur and teacher because it
confirms one aspect of his nature and also because it
is what his parents expect and want. Gabe Wallach,
Alexander Portnoy, David Kepesh, and Zuckerman
all choose a "respectable" vocation in their early attempts both to please their parents and to reward
with success the side of themselves that identifies with
parental values. Zuckerman indicates that his parents
are "awestruck" by the eminence of his position, even
though they provided the model for the characteristics
that have brought him success:

In fact, the example of my own tireless and resolute parents had so instilled in me the habits that make for success
that I had hardly any understanding of failure. Why *did*
people fail? . . . all you had to be was attentive, methodical . . . patient, self-disciplined, undiscourageable, and
industrious—and, of course, intelligent. . . . What could be
simpler?

This formula for success works for the professor until
he finds his orderly world shattered by the emotional
needs of the rake. Then self-discipline and intelli-
gence are of little assistance.

Zuckerman, unwilling to attribute the "catastrophe" that befalls him to the fact that he chafed against the bit of professorial restraint, blames literature for his undoing. The disaster that "ruins" his life, as he phrases it, is his involvement with Lydia Ketterer, a student in his creative writing class. She is five years his senior and not particularly attractive to him sexually; but after vowing to himself, in his stuffy way, to suppress anything extraneous to the "pedagogical transaction" between teacher and student, Zuckerman seduces Lydia. He does so, he suggests, because she has survived "every brand of barbarity" and has proven indestructible; this gives her a kind of "moral stature" to which Nathan, trained in the literature of moral seriousness, responds. Under the influence of fiction and literary criticism, he enters into an affair with her and then a marriage that smacks more of soap opera than high art. However, Zuckerman's final analysis of what he perceives to be the problem that literature has caused him indicates some recognition that he may be partially responsible for his suffering: "It seems that literature too strongly influences my ideas about life, or that I am able to make no connection at all between its wisdom and my existence."

As in *Letting Go,* "Courting Disaster" ends with the protagonist in exile from America, ruminating upon the rash decisions that changed his life. Lydia has committed suicide, and Zuckerman has taken as his lover her rather lame-brained daughter Monica, or "Moonie." He has the sense that he is "living *someone else's life*" because his is so foreign to the life of dignity and regularity that he had planned for himself as an earnest young academic. The choices he has made have transformed Zuckerman just as surely as Kepesh's physical metamorphosis changed him. Reflecting on his marriage to Lydia, Zuckerman suggests that he has "squandered" his manhood; but as Zucker-man-Tarnopol's autobiographical account indicates, he has only begun to learn the lessons of manhood. Like so many of Roth's stories, *My Life as a Man,* taken in its entirety, shows that it is the job of the rake to force upon the professor the kinds of experiences that can make him fully, less innocently, human and enable him to expand his definition of himself to include human as well as humane behavior.

In the last segment of *My Life as a Man,* Roth has Peter Tarnopol propose to abandon artistic contrivances—hold his "imagination at bay"—in order to describe without artifice the marriage that had been the subject of his art. As the preface to the confession, "My True Story," indicates, Tarnopol has undertaken the writing of his memoir after both art and psychoanalysis have failed to unburden him of his obsession with the disaster that "surprised" him at the age of twenty-seven. His "useful fictions" have not done their anticipated work in clarifying his life, and he now turns to "fact" to "demystify" the relationship that has left him troubled and confused.

Once into the process of translating his life into words, however, Tarnopol discovers that his memoir is taking on the characteristics of another useful fiction—that the self he wants to describe with such fidelity is beginning to seem as imaginary as his Zuckermans. Through Tarnopol's realization that even fact takes on the coloration of fiction when it is verbalized, Roth raises the old novelistic question of authorial credibility: Is Tarnopol a more reliable narrator than Zuckerman merely because he has abandoned the trappings of fiction? Roth may also be venting himself a little against his own critics—who suggest that he does not put enough distance between his experiences and his fiction—by emphasizing that the very act of using and ordering words serves to distance the narra-

tive from the thing being narrated. Tarnopol's frustration, and perhaps Roth's defense, is that "words only
approximate the real thing."

In part, what Tarnopol seeks to clarify for himself
in his memoir is his motivation for marrying and then
maintaining a tortuous relationship with the violent
Maureen Johnson. At one point he asks his psychoanalyst, Dr. Spielvogel: "Why should someone with
my devotion to 'seriousness' and 'maturity' knuckle
under like a defenseless little boy to this cornball
Clytemnestra?" Spielvogel suggests that Tarnopol is a
narcissist who derives satisfaction from his "sense of
victimized innocence"; but Tarnopol prefers to think
that it is his sense of earnestness and morality that
caused and perpetuates his predicament, and he
traces these qualities to their origins in literature. Recalling his decision to marry Maureen, who claimed
at the time to be pregnant, Tarnopol thinks that literature and his responsiveness to it were to blame for his
acquiescing to her demands:

Perhaps if I had not fallen in love with these complicated
fictions of moral anguish, I never would have taken that
long anguished walk to the Upper West Side and back,
and arrived at what seemed to me the only "honorable"
decision for a young man as morally "serious" as myself.

Tarnopol tends to believe that he is suffering
what Mark Shechner has called "the English major's
fate"—to be "done in by the tight-lipped moralism of
the great Protestant tradition and by those ideas
about honor, duty, and manly responsibility" that are
the mainstay of a literary education.[7]

This view that the "civilized" professor marries a
loathsome woman because he seeks in his life the
earnestness of experiences portrayed in fiction is accurate only to a point. It does not take into account
the motivations of the rakish element—the part of

Tarnopol that admits to liking "something taxing" in his love affairs, "something problematical and puzzling to keep the imagination going" when he is away from his books. In the early stages of their relationship, Tarnopol considers Maureen a challenge—a "rough customer"—and is attracted to her as the embodiment of potential disorder in his life. It may be, as Melvin Maddocks suggests, that Maureen represents the "muse of disorder, the Dionysian element every artist suspects he needs." [8] But only the rake would recognize and respond to her as such. The professor, "stuffed to the gills with great fiction," as Tarnopol describes his premarital self, prefers the distance and order of art to the immediacy and chaos of life. The rake, however, will not settle for a hothouse existence. He wants to be "stuffed to the gills" with emotional and sexual experience. And, as Tarnopol soon learns, while this experience becomes a resource for the artist, it is almost more than the man can handle.

Curiously enough, Maureen, whom Tarnopol presents as completely lacking in sensitivity, sees herself as a potential muse to Tarnopol. In her journal, the one place in "My True Story" where she is revealed directly, Maureen records her analysis of the activating role she has played in Tarnopol's life and indicates that if it were not for her, Tarnopol would still be hiding in his books, not knowing real life "if he fell over it." "What," she asks, "did he think he was going to write *about*, knowing and believing nothing but what he read in books?" Maureen may be justifying her own behavior, but she is also making a case for the necessity of the Dionysian element in the production of art. She concludes that she could be Tarnopol's muse if only he would let her. Ironically, she is more of a muse than she knows, for it is his relationship with her that activates Tarnopol's imagination and causes him to work and rework his life and, in the process, to refine his theories about art.

Because Tarnopol, unlike most of Roth's other professor-rake protagonists, has to deal with his conflicted nature in terms of his art as well as his life, *My Life as a Man* extends the professor-rake metaphor into aesthetics. It poses the problem of the kind of artistic mode best suited for transforming personal experience into art and, through Tarnopol, shows the artist's difficulties in achieving detachment from his material. Tarnopol is continuously torn between a desire to tell his story with the kind of control and distance he has always admired in writers like Flaubert and the suspicion that what he is trying to express in his "true story" is better suited to the coarser, more confessional modes of Henry Miller and Céline.[9]

Tarnopol's professorial nature prefers the dignified reserve of Flaubert, since he can never see himself as a "renegade bohemian or cut up of any kind" (the professor's notion of Miller and Céline). Yet he knows that what he is doing is not just art; it is also self-exposure to a degree and self-explanation. The irony is that his self-exposure is not candid enough to be in a class with Miller's or Céline's. Thus, in his art as in his personal life, Tarnopol functions somewhere in between two alternative modes. Just as he is not fully a professor, a rake, or a harmonious blending of the two, so his fictions follow neither Flaubert nor Miller—nor do they have an authenticity of their own that satisfies him. When he suggests that he is "too much 'under the sway of passion' for Flaubertian transcendence, but too raw and touchy by far . . . for a full-scale unbuttoning à la Henry Miller," Tarnopol indicates the limbo in which he, as both man and artist, exists. The only solution the artist can find is to tell the man's story over and over again with the hope that all three—artist, man, and story—will become comprehensible.

But if there is anything Tarnopol wants more than to understand himself as an artist, it is to understand himself as a man. As the title indicates, *My Life as a Man* is concerned with male identity, and it explores the meaning of the word "man" in its several variations—manhood, manliness, humanity. The novel also links the problematical question of manhood to the professor-rake conflict. In contrast to Portnoy, however, for Tarnopol being "a man" is not mainly a matter of sexual conquest; it also involves asserting his autonomy in a relationship with a woman. The professor finds this hard to do. When Tarnopol asks himself, "How do I ever get to be what is described in the literature as *a man*?" he is not referring to sexual liberty so much as the freedom to act without fear of reprisal from women. He wants to be powerful, confident, and self-controlled rather than what he says he is—the "Dagwood Bumstead of fear and trembling."

Although Tarnopol finds manhood difficult to achieve, in him the Roth hero finally makes some headway in recognizing the link between male and female autonomy—or lack of it—when he sees that one of the reasons for his failure to attain a satisfactory degree of "manly" independence lies in his involvement with pitifully dependent women. Because Maureen cannot be whole and free, she does everything she can to shackle Tarnopol and thus almost destroys his hopes for autonomy and freedom for himself. He is being victimized by Maureen because she herself has been victimized by a society that trains women to be helpless and inept. Her only weapon for survival becomes the mask of impotent defiance that she wears to cover "her ineptitude and desperation."

As Tarnopol begins to understand this, he realizes that Maureen's predicament (and his) is common to most women in relationship to men. She and the other women in his life are victims of a "virus to which only a few women among us are immune." Finally, Tarnopol is convinced that there is nothing he can do to free either himself or Maureen from the bind that societal roles and socially sanctioned patterns of victimization have forced upon them. Even the symbolic surrender of masculinity implied in his wearing Maureen's clothes does nothing to mitigate the enmity between them. Tarnopol wants to be "good" and "reasonable," and he also wants to be "humanish: manly, a man"; but he is caught in a situation that seems to make those attributes impossible.

My Life as a Man concludes with Maureen's death in an automobile accident, but since this is not the chronological ending of Tarnopol's story, it is apparent that her death does not free him. He has already dealt with the death fictionally in "Courting Disaster" and earlier in "My True Story." When Spielvogel tells Tarnopol, "You have been released," he has chosen his words well. Tarnopol has been "released" from Maureen, but freedom is something he will have to achieve for himself. Even his best imaginative effort cannot yet project the optimistic conclusion to his story.

The Professor of Desire

When Roth next takes up the theme of the duality of restraint and passion, high-minded moral responsibility and sensuous self-assertion, he allows the novel's title to communicate the conflicting elements. *The Professor of Desire* is Roth's most direct presentation of the struggles, defeats, and triumphs of a man attempting to reconcile the serious and moral aspects of himself, which are manifested in his profession, with the lustful and adventuresome side, which urges him to defy restriction and convention. Here Roth returns to the cast of *The Breast,* expanding the character of the protagonist and rounding out several of the supporting characters. He is still concerned with Kepesh's transformation, but this time it is a psychic rather than a physical one. Kepesh becomes the first of Roth's protagonists to make the transition from professor-rake to "conscientious" professor.

Roth focuses a considerable portion of the novel on Kepesh's childhood and early experiences as a "sexual prodigy" in much the same way that he detailed Portnoy's early life; but here the parents are not depicted as the perpetrators of the protagonist's problems. It is apparent that the seeds of Kepesh's later conflicts are buried within the character of the innocent David Kepesh. From childhood, he wants to be good, to accomplish something worthwhile, and to please his adoring parents; but the lure of the forbidden is there. Kepesh's childhood prototype for "shameless exhibitionism" is the bawdy, itinerant entertainer Herbie Bratasky, whose hipster appearance and "lavatory imitations" mesmerize the pure young boy. Bratasky represents one of the earliest and most memorable temptations to adventure in young Kepesh's life.

Like the other professors, Kepesh grows into a young overachieving academic moralist; but he soon recognizes the other side of his character—the side that once was attracted to the Bratasky brashness and now longs for erotic sexual and interpersonal adventure. He continuously attempts to achieve the balance that he had in childhood, when life in his parents' Catskill resort was divided between orderly, peaceful winters and chaotic, stimulating summers; but his conflicting desires begin to create for him a "dilemma of insuperable moral proportions." Finally, he finds in two literary aphorisms a way to resolve his dilemma temporarily. He proposes to become, like Steele, a "rake among scholars, a scholar among rakes" and to follow the Byronic dictum of being "studious by day, dissolute by night." In this way, he intends to have the best of both worlds and to indulge rake and scholar alike.

Temporarily armed with a justification for gratifying both mind and body, Kepesh sets off for London for what is supposed to be a year of graduate study; but even before he attends his first lecture on Icelandic poetry, he discovers the sexual pleasures that the Shepherd Market section of London has to offer. His year of study turns into a year of full-time debauchery with two Swedish adventurers, Birgitta and Elizabeth; the scholar and his Fulbright go by the wayside as the rake has his day. But the conflict, which manifests itself as guilt and fear of impotence, surfaces occasionally even in Kepesh's year of pleasure. After a particularly vigorous workout with Birgitta, he says: "I had been fearful that it might be decades before I was potent again, that my punishment, if such it was, might last forever." It does not last forever, but impotence (and the fear of it) is a specter that continues to haunt Kepesh and most of the other professors. In *Portnoy's Complaint*, *The Breast*, *My Life as a Man*, and *The Professor of Desire*, impotence becomes the revenge that the professor takes on the rake when the rake goes too far (for the professor, at least).

After a time of playing the "precocious dramatist of the satyric and the lewd," Kepesh suddenly calls a halt to his adventure. His professorial inclinations beckon him back to serious pursuits and discipline; and, unconvinced that it is his nature to be a "shameless carnal force," he decides to try becoming the scholar. When Kepesh finally breaks with Birgitta to return to Stanford to complete his Ph.D., the third-person narrator steps in to predict further conflicts for the protagonist:

Yes, easily as that do young Birgitta Svanstrom and young David Kepesh rid themselves of each other. Ridding himself of what he is *by nature* may be a more difficult task, however, since young Kepesh does not appear to be that clear, quite yet, as to what his nature is, exactly.

Kepesh returns to the United States convinced that if he is to accomplish anything in life, he will have to restrain that side of himself which seems to be "strongly susceptible to the most bewildering and debilitating sort of temptations." He has begun to learn the difficulty of following the maxims that at age twenty seemed so applicable. Far from being able to balance the embattled tendencies within a twenty-four-hour day, Kepesh finds that he can indulge one extreme only by restraining the other. He is cyclically either scholar or rake but not yet an amalgam of the two.

The professorial Kepesh manages to keep everything under control until, like many of Roth's protagonists, he is forced to face his own duality in relationship to a woman. By challenging his studied detachment and control, Helen Baird (another of Roth's "handfuls") propels Kepesh into the next phase of his initiation into his own character. Helen is a worldly, unpredictable, uncontrollable adventurer who represents everything Kepesh knows he *should* avoid but cannot quite resist. She is reminiscent of Maureen Tarnopol in her preference for life over literature and in her way of challenging the illusions that the protagonist has learned from literature. "Look," she says to Kepesh early in their relationship, "so there is no confusion, let me only mildly overstate the case: I hate libraries, I hate books, and I hate schools. As I remember, they tend to turn everything about life into something slightly other than it is." That is exactly what she thinks literature has done to Kepesh—turned him into something "slightly other" than he is, a little bit of a lie.

Kepesh's involvement with Helen and finally his marriage to her result from much the same confusion of emotions that Tarnopol experienced with Maureen. Helen,[10] as her name implies, is more the beautiful enchantress than Maureen; but she, too, has a tragic background, an exotic and dangerous past, that draws her lover perhaps as much as anything else. For a time, Kepesh finds in her an escape from the rigidity and boredom of his scholarly life, but eventually the very qualities that attracted him to Helen make their relationship a torment.

Kepesh begins to take refuge in the old professorial pleasures—working sixteen hours a day teaching his classes and writing a book on "romantic disillusionment in the stories of Anton Chekhov." [11] Helen spends her time at her toilette, indulging her body and refusing to see life in terms of lamb chops and balanced checkbooks. Finally each of them, as Kepesh says, "has been reduced to precisely what the other had been so leery of at the outset, the professorial 'smugness' and 'prissiness' for which Helen detests me with all her heart . . . no less in evidence than her 'utter mindlessness,' 'idiotic wastefulness,' 'adolescent dreaminess,' etc." Not unpredictably, the marriage ends in divorce; and while Kepesh does not experience Tarnopol's difficulties in getting "released" from his marriage, he does experience a similar problem in freeing himself from the effects of the relationship.

Once more in the annals of the "nice Jewish boy" recorded by Roth, the protagonist makes his way to the psychoanalyst's couch to confess all and to find relief from his suffering at the skirt of a woman. Dr.

Frederick Klinger, Kepesh's psychoanalyst in *The Breast,* returns in this episode to assist Kepesh in his attempts to immunize himself against "Hong Kong Helen." During the sessions with Dr. Klinger, Kepesh tries to formulate a philosophy that will clarify the realities of intimacy and reconcile the old emotional conflicts; and he begins to gain some insight into his own internal struggle when he sees it objectified and polarized in the personalities of two of his colleagues. His department chairman, Arthur Schonbrunn, epitomizes the limitations of the professor; the poet, Ralph Baumgarten, demonstrates the risks and joys that come to the lusty rake.

Schonbrunn, whom Kepesh describes as a "handsome and exquisitely groomed middle-aged man of unflagging charm and punctiliousness," becomes a parody of the proper, conforming professor. Baumgarten, on the other hand, is portrayed as a larger-than-life rake who tries to jump all the boundaries of propriety and decency. Kepesh comes to see him as his "secret sharer," his alter ego, but only in the sense that Baumgarten represents the kind of person he might be if he did not have that other voice inside him "Schonbrunning" him into submission. Again, Kepesh's problem is clear: he can be neither Schonbrunn nor Baumgarten nor a comfortable mix of the two. His deepest desire is to be a Kepesh, "with his mouth frothing and his long tongue lolling, leash slipped and running wild," but guilt, fear, and uncertainty always call him back to the "kennels."

Kepesh's breakdown and the sessions with Dr. Klinger raise many of the recurring questions in Roth's novels: Is love necessary? Why are love and intimacy so difficult? Has the protagonist been too sensible or too sensual? This section of the novel in which Kepesh attempts to resolve his problems through analysis sifts through all the old insolubilities of the professor-rake conflict. Yet this time, the protagonist's relationship with his aging parents broadens the familiar dilemma and suggests that it exists within the context of mortality and death. At last, the professor-rake begins to realize that he does not have forever to resolve the problems of relationship. His mother's death and his father's diminishing life make Kepesh aware of the limitations of time. To the worn-out and unanswered questions of love and identity he must now add new and more disturbing ones: How long does he have to solve these problems? Is it too late—or almost too late? Kepesh's growing awareness of the grim reality of the human condition is reiterated in the conclusion of a composition on Chekhov in which one of his students observes: "We are born innocent . . . we suffer terrible disillusionment before we can gain knowledge, and then we fear death—and we are granted only fragmentary happiness to offset the pain."

That reality is one that Kepesh has to confront repeatedly; but after his sessions with Dr. Klinger, he is granted fragmentary happiness in a relationship with Claire Ovington, the very antithesis of Helen. Claire is a schoolteacher with a proclivity for rationality and order, and under her "program" of kindness and comfort, the professor mellows. Not more than a year later, however, the rake begins to find the regularity monotonous. Traveling with Claire in Italy, Kepesh recalls his youthful adventures with the uninhibited Birgitta and feels a "surging sense of lascivious kinship" with the woman of his memories. He manages to recover from this mental lapse in fidelity to Claire, but even as he temporarily renews his old enthusiasm for her, he expresses his relationship with Claire in decidedly ambiguous terms. "Once again," he says, "I feel I am being sealed up in something wonderful." Despite the word "wonderful," being "sealed up" suggests that Kepesh views his stable and pre-

dictable life with Claire as entrapment—the most negative symbol in the novel.

Kepesh and Claire end their vacation in the Cats-
kills, not far from where Kepesh spent his peaceful
boyhood. By now, however, he has learned that no
peace is enduring, and he is already mentally pre-
paring himself for the demise of what has temporarily
been a restorative relationship with Claire. Kepesh
has not been able to solve the problem of character
that haunts him and disrupts his life. The conflict per-
sists, the result is a painful loss of relationship, and all
he can do is grieve about it.

Already it is dying and I am afraid that there is nothing
I can do to save it. . . . To be robbed like this of you. And
of this life I love and have hardly gotten to know! And
robbed by whom? It always comes down to myself.

Finally, the Roth protagonist sees that he himself is
the problem and realizes that because the conflict is
inherent in him, he can never resolve it. He is no longer
blaming other people, as Portnoy does, or suffering in
panic like Tarnopol. Grief is the professor-rake's mature and realistic response to the losses incurred by
his own nature.

The Professor of Desire ends pessimistically, recalling the lament for the loss of innocence and happiness in the student's theme. Kepesh lies beside
Claire at night, dreading the "transformations yet to
come"—the loss of their love and the death of his
father. It is apparent that in this novel Roth is no
longer (if he ever was) writing simply about the
identity struggles of his characters. He is writing
about the human condition—the transformations from
innocence to experience, from idealism to disillusionment—and those fragmentary moments of happiness
which offset the pain.

If in this case Roth carries his protagonist deeper

into the experience of conflict than before, he also offers him greater consolation. Only Kepesh among Roth's professor-rakes realizes fully the legitimate rewards of literature and finds a way to "use" it (as Tarnopol, for all his "useful" fictions, cannot) to gain perspective on his life. He is especially drawn to the fiction of Chekhov and Kafka, finding in their stories evidence of a universal struggle between license and restraint that has particular significance for him. At one point, he writes an analysis of Chekhov's work that serves the dual purpose of helping him understand his own situation and enabling Roth to guide the reader toward an understanding of Kepesh. The essay, called "Man in a Shell" after a Chekhov story of the same name, deals with oppressive conformity in Chekhov's fictional world. But for Kepesh the problem is more than fictional, for he sees reflected in the stories his own very real entrapment in the conflict between conformity and freedom. And he finds his fate tragically forecast in the humiliations, failures, and destructiveness of those characters who

seek a way *out* of the shell of restrictions and convention, out of the pervasive boredom and the stifling despair, out of the painful marital situations and the endemic social falsity, into what they take to be a vibrant and desirable life.

Ultimately, Kepesh's Chekhov study echoes the message that reverberates throughout *The Professor of Desire*—that both longings and pleasure occasion pain because both are uncertain and both end. Roth's stories and Chekhov's tell of men and women who fail to achieve "that sense of personal freedom" to which both writers are devoted as the problematical subject of their fiction. Like the characters in Chekhov, Roth's professor-rake never fully resolves the conflict between restraint and freedom. Because the fate of the Roth protagonist is determined ultimately by the very nature of his character, "personal freedom" remains an illusion.

Chekhov's work assists Kepesh in identifying his problems, but it is the influence of Kafka that helps him realize that they can be borne and that literature relieves the burden. On his memorial visit to Kafka's grave, Kepesh encounters and has an extensive conversation with a man identified only as Professor Soska. He turns out to be a deposed Czech literature teacher who has been reduced to professional and political impotence by the Communist takeover of his country. He is also a devotee of Kafka, and he tells Kepesh that for him and others like him, life is made bearable by devotion to the memory of this great writer of literature.

Deprived of his profession and his freedom, Soska bases his life on the example of Kafka's tolerance for an existence of futility, impotence, and frustration. Instead of killing himself opposing the regime in control, he takes refuge, even joy, in attempting to translate Melville's *Moby Dick* into Czech. It is a task, he explains, that he knows to be useless, but somehow the very fact that it will not be published invigorates rather than debilitates him. The writing project provides him with a way of sublimating his rage, just as the example of Kafka offers a means of living with obstruction. What he tries to teach Kepesh is that literature can offer prototypes for survival and become an outlet for emotion. When Kepesh wonders what bookish people are to do with all the great prose they read, Soska replies: "sink their teeth into it. . . . Into the books, instead of into the hand that throttles them."

The difficulty for Kepesh in following Soska's advice is that the "hand that throttles" him is his own. Attempting to see his situation in light of Soska's, he says: "I can only compare the body's utter single-mindedness, its cold indifference and absolute contempt for the well-being of the spirit, to some unyielding, authoritarian regime." His flesh dominates his spirit just as surely as the Communist regime dominates Soska. But Kepesh's enemy is within; and if literature is a grace for living, it must lead him to make peace between his warring selves.

The lecture that he prepares for his course in comparative literature indicates that if the professor and the rake have not made peace, they have at least called a truce. This Kepesh in the classroom will not be the earlier professor, seeking in literature a refuge from life; rather, he proposes to use literature to confront life. He will become, if only for a time, the conscientious professor. Kepesh has learned, and wants to teach, that literature is essentially "referential"— that it is located in the world of experience and has reference to, and significance for, the experiences of its readers. Urging his students to avoid the jargon of criticism, he emphasizes that the value of fiction transcends "structure" and "symbol"—that it can teach "something of value about life in one of its most puzzling and maddening aspects."

Since the course has been structured to focus on erotic desire, that is the "puzzling and maddening" aspect of life to which Kepesh refers and which he has experienced firsthand. He will teach novels that deal with desire, he will give an account of his own erotic history, and he will confront the most puzzling aspect of his nature. What he proposes, in essence, is that the professor draw upon the experiences of the rake in order to teach authoritatively; at the same time, the professor will be tutoring the rake in the "universal" manifestations of his drives and compulsions. The liaison between the two polarities is to be literature; and the result is Kepesh the "conscientious

professor," denying neither side of his nature. The concluding words of his lecture illustrate his acceptance
of both professor and rake, at least intellectually: "I
am devoted to fiction, and I assure you that in time I
will tell you whatever I may know about it, but in
truth nothing lives in me like my life."

The first half or so of *The Professor of Desire* is
typical Roth, reminiscent in some ways of *Portnoy's
Complaint* and *My Life as a Man* in its depiction
of David Kepesh's young manhood and marriage. The
sardonic tone that often characterizes Roth's portrayal
of the rake's excesses and the professor's moral seriousness, particularly as it has been imbibed from literature, is there. In the second half of the book, however, Roth allows Kepesh the consolations of literature,
without mocking and without implying that a fondness
for art is necessarily a retreat from life. Kepesh discovers, because Roth allows him to, that although the
resolution of interpersonal, erotic, and existential conflicts is impossible, through literature they can be understood—or at least expressed and perhaps sublimated.

The Ghost Writer

In his latest book, *The Ghost Writer,* Roth returns to
the problems of artistic authenticity he had explored
in *My Life as a Man* and to a protagonist called
Nathan Zuckerman; but here old problems take on a
fresh perspective as Roth subordinates the difficulties
of human relationships to the primary question, What
must the artist *be* in order to create authentically?
This question still involves what in previous novels is
the professor-rake conflict; but it shifts the emphasis
from professor-rake as lover, where the conflict is most
evident in his relationships with women, to professor-
rake as artist, where the choices can be seen primarily

in terms of the various ways of living that are conducive to creativity.

The novella is cast in the form of an artistic pilgrimage, as Nathan Zuckerman, a twenty-three-year-old Jewish fiction writer in search of a mentor, makes his way to the home of the revered E. I. Lonoff, an established Jewish writer. Zuckerman makes this journey seeking to clarify his ambitions and identity as a writer, but he also wants a father surrogate who will give him approval for being who he is and writing what he writes. After several novels in which the difficulties of relationship are expressly between men and women, Roth returns to the problems inherent in the father-son relationship. Consequently, Zuckerman looks to Lonoff for validation as both artist and son.

As he did in *The Professor of Desire*, Roth objectifies here the split between the professor and the rake in two different personalities. Lonoff as artist exemplifies the order and control of the professor. His counterpart is another older writer whom Zuckerman admires, Felix Abravanel. It is to Lonoff's mode of living, however, that the young artist is particularly attracted; and when Zuckerman visits Lonoff in his rural New York retreat, he thinks: "Purity. Serenity. Simplicity. Seclusion. All one's concentration and flamboyance and originality reserved for the gruelling, exalted, transcendent calling. I looked around and I thought, This is how I will live."

Lonoff, however, seems to have no illusions about the extent to which his orderliness and control have limited both his life and his art. He implies that for him, writing has become reducible to rule, merely a matter of "turning sentences around"; and yet if he abandons that orderly routine, unimaginative as it may be, he becomes "frantic with boredom and a sense of waste." His distance and his devotion have also affected adversely his relationship to those about him. In the segment of the book called "Married to Tolstoy," Hope Lonoff finally expresses her frustrations with her husband's methodical way of approaching his life and with his art when she erupts with the bitterness of thirty-five years of catering to his caution: "There is his religion of art . . . rejecting life! *Not* living is what he makes his beautiful fiction *out* of!"

The other possible prototype for the kind of life that Zuckerman can make his fiction "out of" is represented by Felix Abravanel. He is popular and extroverted, an exhibitionist in his life and his art. Even Lonoff appreciates the passion and energy that are so different from his own reserve: "Like him? No. But impressed, oh, yes. Absolutely. It's no picnic up there in the egosphere. I don't know when the man sleeps, or if he has ever slept, aside from those few minutes when he had that drink with me." Abravanel's books forgo subtlety to show "mankind aflame with feeling"; in contrast to Lonoff, he is—as man and artist—clearly identifiable as the expansive, self-indulgent rake.

The first section of *The Ghost Writer* shows Zuckerman attempting to make some decisions about the kind of identity most facilitating for an artist and asking himself whether he wants to model his future on the disciplined, domestic Lonoff or the flamboyant, lecherous Abravanel. Predictably, Roth implies that the maturation of the artist requires an acceptance of the expansive, rakish qualities as well as professorial control and commitment. This section of the book, called "Maestro," ends with Zuckerman's responding positively to the fastidious Lonoff and remembering his childhood affection for his father.

The father-son conflict, which is partially responsible for Zuckerman's search for mentors and models in the "Maestro" section, dominates the next segment, "Nathan Dedalus." Here Roth, still examining the artistic role and identity of the writer, pursues the writer's relationship to his past—his roots in the family and culture. Young Zuckerman experiences the usual discord inherent in parent-child relationships, but he is also troubled by the added disharmony that is the consequence of a bourgeois father's inability to understand his "artistic" son. This problem is compounded by Mr. Zuckerman's reaction to the kinds of stories his son writes, which he believes to be disparaging of Jews. He takes the position that many of Roth's Jewish critics have—that for a writer to portray Jews in a less-than-ideal way is to encourage anti-Semitism and, possibly, help foster a climate dangerous for Jews. Nathan's disappointment over his father's inability to accept the distinction that he makes between life and art is complicated by the love he feels for his father. Love, however, turns to shame and anger when Mr. Zuckerman elicits the help of the influential Judge Wapter, who urges Nathan to see the Broadway production of "The Diary of Anne Frank" and heed its message.

During the night he spends at Lonoff's, Zuckerman finds himself eavesdropping on Lonoff and his protégée Amy, who are engaged in a conversation that implies sexual intimacy as well as filial devotion. Falling asleep at last, Zuckerman dreams of Amy in a way that connects his troubled relationship to his father with his concern for his validity as an artist. In the dream, Amy is a disguised Anne Frank who has survived the Holocaust and come to America to escape her grim past. She believes that the rest of her family is dead until she learns that her father has lived to publish her diary. Although there is a personal emphasis in the dream that connects Amy-Anne Frank's ambivalence toward her aging father with Zuckerman's, the dream also alludes to the conflicts that the twentieth-century Jewish writer experiences

in terms of a paternal culture that links him to a
past that includes centuries of persecution—and the
Holocaust.

Through Zuckerman's artistic pilgrimage, Roth
again seems to be defending his own integrity as a
writer. Ever since his earliest critics attacked him on
much the same grounds that Mr. Zuckerman and
Wapter use against Nathan, Roth has been trying to
explain to his readers what he considers to be the
proper relationship between his Jewishness and his
art. Here, Amy-Anne Frank relinquishes her father's
love and seems to put aside the horrors of the
Holocaust in order to live her life and allow her art
to serve its purpose. Both Amy-Anne and Zuckerman
make the decisions they do because they value their
artistic gifts—not because they reject or misunderstand
their Jewishness. Finally, the dream (and Lonoff's
words echo the theme) suggests that the artist has no
choice—he must be who he is in order to create. As
Zuckerman tells his father: "I *am* the kind of person
who writes this kind of story!" Similarly, Amy-Anne
concludes that "if she is going to be exceptional, it
would not be because of Auschwitz and Belsen but
because of what she had made of herself since." For
Amy, "the time will come when we are people again,
and not just Jews." Nevertheless, both are torn by
guilt and loneliness as they separate themselves from
a past that includes their fathers, their families, and
their heritage. By the time Roth writes *The Professor
of Desire* and *The Ghost Writer,* his protagonists are
no longer struggling with the failed and ineffectual
fathers of *Portnoy's Complaint* and *Letting Go.* Now
they realize that, for the sake of their work and their
own manhood, they must separate themselves from
powerful, loving fathers—who happen to be different
from themselves.

Although the story ends with an argument be-

tween the Lonoffs in which Hope Lonoff summarizes
the worst possibilities for the professor-artist so obsessed with order and style that he rejects all change
and thus all human involvement, the last few lines
contain a blessing from Lonoff and a reiteration of his
belief that Zuckerman is to become a writer different
from himself: "I'll be curious to see how we all come
out someday [in the fictional version of his visit that
he thinks Zuckerman will write]. It could be an interesting story. You're not so nice and polite in your
fiction. . . . You're a different person." Zuckerman thus
gets from Lonoff what he had wanted from his father—permission to be the kind of person and the kind
of writer that he must be, the artist-professor whose
works are enriched by the experiences of the rake.

In *The Ghost Writer*, Zuckerman's artistic pilgrimage ends when Lonoff administers his "rites of
confirmation." Yet the conclusion of the book makes
clear that Zuckerman's journey is just beginning and
leaves the reader curious about the kind of writer he
will become. Apparently, Roth intends to satisfy the
reader's curiosity. He has indicated in a letter to one
of the authors (September 18, 1980) that his next
book, which is to be published in June of 1981, will be
called *Zuckerman Unbound* and will portray Nathan
Zuckerman thirteen years after the episodes detailed
in *The Ghost Writer*.

3

○○

Roth's Satire:
Sheer Playfulness
and Deadly Seriousness

In 1974, when the novelist Joyce Carol Oates re-
marked on the shift from seriousness in *Letting Go*
and *When She Was Good* to "playfulness" in *Our
Gang* and *The Great American Novel,* Roth rejected
the implication that a categorical opposition existed
between his "moral" and his "comic" works. "Sheer
Playfulness and Deadly Seriousness," he said, were
both his "closest friends." In his writing, these two
intimates of Roth's coexist most companionably in
the satire that reflects his disillusionment with the
"Great American Dream." All his books, "comic" or
"moral," challenge simplistic notions of society, religion, and human relationships; but *Our Gang, The
Great American Novel,* and some of the short stories
best demonstrate Roth's disappointment with failed
American ideals. In these works, in which the focus is
primarily sociopolitical rather than psychological, Roth
plays with language and with form; but he is also
deadly serious in his satiric intent to reveal the perversions in American reality.

Early in his career, Roth published an essay
called "Writing American Fiction" that has become
seminal to criticism of recent American literature. In
it, he describes the position of the novelist in the mid-
twentieth century and points to the reasons for the

satiric orientation of much of his fiction. Taking a
bizarre news story about the murder of two Chicago
girls as an example of the way actuality has become
more incredible than fiction, Roth suggests that contemporary American life and values almost defy fictional representation. The novelist finds it nearly impossible to represent a culture that is too crazy and
values that are too distorted to be believed. As a consequence, he begins to feel disenfranchised from the
culture that in its everyday reality outstrips his imagination; and, as Roth suggests, "for a writer of fiction
to feel that he does not really live in his own country . . . must seem a serious occupational impediment." It is particularly an impediment because, as
Roth makes clear, the writer needs a valid sense of
community in order to work. When his community
becomes unacceptable—or fantastical—to him, he is
left in the position of an insider who must view the
world as if from the outside. Finally, without a legitimate sense of community, the novelist faces a loss of
subject that amounts to a loss of vocation. It is his
task to present a version of reality, but doing so is
increasingly difficult when reality becomes distorted
to the point of unbelievability. The loss of a subject,
the difficulty of writing credibly about the times, Roth
maintains, has led in American fiction to a "voluntary
withdrawal of interest by the fiction writer from some
of the grander social and political phenomena of our
times."

These comments about the grotesqueries of the
American social and political scene help explain the
reasons for the extravagant nature of some of Roth's
experiments—*Portnoy, The Breast, Our Gang,* and
The Great American Novel. For if the subject is distorted beyond belief, the literature that attempts to
represent it will be equally distorted; and if the

reality is strange enough, the fiction is apt to seem absurd. According to Roth,

the American writer in the middle of the twentieth century has his hands full in trying to understand, describe, and then make credible much of American reality. . . . The actuality is continually outdoing our talents, and the culture tosses up figures almost daily that are the envy of any novelist.

Instead of spurning the world of American reality, however, Roth attempts to confront it imaginatively—and often through satire that for all its comic extravagances is serious. He has said that "in satire it is *by* kidding around that one hopes to reveal just *how* serious" a subject is; he has defined satire as "moral rage transformed into comic art." Consequently, in Roth's hands caricature, parody, burlesque, and other comic devices serve as the vehicles by which he makes a serious assault upon the American experience.

The satiric thrust of Roth's writing has been apparent since the earliest stories. *Goodbye, Columbus,* in the title piece and the shorter stories, attacks the shallowness of contemporary standards, in which material and social success takes precedence over spiritual and interpersonal values. *Letting Go* and *When She Was Good,* though hardly comic in intention and therefore outside Roth's definition of satire, both expose moral tyranny, the rigidity of middle-class values, and the inadequacies of American family life. *Portnoy's Complaint* relies on the devices of parody, burlesque, and hyperbole; although Roth is cautious about calling it a satire, preferring to characterize it as a "satirical lament," the novel ultimately derides Portnoy as the self-designated victim of a "Jewish joke" at the same time that it exposes the social reality behind the joke.

The impetus for much of Roth's satire is his realization of the incongruity between American ideals and actuality; and the disillusioning discovery of this disparity comes to most of his characters in one way or another. Usually, it is only one of several harsh realities that the Roth character has to confront; but in "You Can't Tell a Man by the Song He Sings," a story in the *Goodbye, Columbus* volume, the truth behind the American myth of liberty and justice becomes the focal point. The narrator is a typical Roth "good" boy, who loves baseball and means it when he pledges allegiance to the flag. His new acquaintances in his freshman year at high school are former inmates of reform schools. Albie Pelagutti does not even know how to play baseball, and neither he nor his fellow delinquent, Duke Scarpa, believes in the rules of fair play that the narrator thinks govern life in America. They have no illusions to be shattered.

When the three boys are caught fighting and Albie and Duke abandon him, the narrator is shocked by their disloyalty. He is dismayed even further when he learns in the principal's office about the cards that are kept on students and the records of misconduct that will "follow [them] through life." He discovers that "justice for all" is an illusion, that the principal (like society) punishes not according to present behavior but according to the offender's past record. He then realizes that Albie and Duke abandoned him because they knew the realities of the system much better than he did—that justice is not the same thing for "bad" boys as it is for "good" boys.

The irony of the narrator's discovery that society does not forgive—that it just keeps records of an individual's "mistakes"—is accentuated by an incident that provides a corollary to the narrator's experience in the principal's office. He and the other boys in his "Occupations" class play a joke on their teacher, Mr.

Russo, that ends with class and teacher standing to sing the National Anthem. Fifteen years later, this event takes on significance for the narrator when he learns that Mr. Russo has been fired for the alleged Marxist affinities of his college years. The narrator considers coming to his defense by relating the time in the classroom when Mr. Russo had stood and participated in the singing of the "Star-Spangled Banner," but he is uncertain as to how this evidence of the teacher's patriotism will be construed. He finally concludes that it has taken the idealistic teacher even longer than it took him to learn what Albie and Scarpa knew almost from childhood—that society remembers errant behavior and judges accordingly and that the democratic dream of "equal justice" is an illusion, a myth.

This early story reflects the naive disappointment that often seems to be the basis of Roth's satire. Like the narrator of "You Can't Tell a Man by the Song He Sings" and others of his idealistic characters, Roth seems unwilling to believe that the patriotic ideals of parents and teachers are based on falsehoods or that all those people who sing the "Star-Spangled Banner" do not mean what they say in the way he thought they were supposed to. That this same kind of frustrated idealism is behind *Our Gang*, Roth's book-length satire of Richard Nixon and his administration, is apparent when Roth talks about what "triggered" the book. Confessing that he is, "like so many satirists, just a naif at heart," Roth indicates that he was incredulous when Richard Nixon used the power of his office essentially to condone the murdering of unarmed civilians in Vietnam. He had known, he suggests, that Nixon was a "moral ignoramus" and a "scheming opportunist"; but, Roth implies, he was still naive or idealistic enough to believe that even Nixon would not "sink to something like this."

Our Gang

Roth transforms his moral outrage into a scathing
satire that points to the disjunction between the American myth of presidential integrity and the political
reality. As with all Roth's experimental and satiric
works, the critical response to *Our Gang* has been
varied. Some early reviewers described it as a "brilliant protest against the debasement of contemporary
political language" and "the wittiest and wickedest
political satire since Dryden." Others, less impressed
with Roth's first venture into sustained political satire,
called the book "sour humor," an "artistic failure," and
a "dreary interlude" in Roth's career. At times, the book
is witty and funny, with the humor of parody and
exaggeration at which Roth is a master, but often the
humor becomes silly and the exposition monotonous.
Yet even the silliness and the monotony make Roth's
point: Nixon is not only bad; he is foolish and boring
as well. For Roth, it is inevitable that a fatuous,
immoral person express himself in dull, dishonest language. And on another level the subject of the book
is the abuse of language—the manipulation of language so that it confuses rather than clarifies.

Roth reveals the subject and purpose of *Our
Gang* in two introductory passages, one excerpted
from Jonathan Swift's *Gulliver's Travels* and the other
taken from George Orwell's "Politics and the English
Language." [1] The quotation from *Gulliver's Travels*
points up the ubiquity of lying "among human Creatures" and the resulting confusion in meaning and
communication. Obviously, the character Roth labels
Tricky E. Dixon has perfected the art of false representation to the extent that he automatically uses
language to disguise rather than reveal whatever it is
that he considers the truth. He deliberately juggles

language so that it obscures meaning. The Orwell quotation goes even further in suggesting that words and the way they are used reveal not merely meaning but being as well. It foreshadows Roth's demonstration of how language reveals the essence of a personality, even of a government, and leads to the conclusion that the correction of one may correct the other. As Roth says in discussing *Our Gang*: "One ought to recognize that the present political chaos is connected with the decay of language, and that one can probably bring about some improvement by starting at the verbal end."

The satire itself, *Our Gang: (Starring Tricky and His Friends)*, begins with a quotation from a speech made by Richard Nixon on April 3, 1971. In it he reveals his attitude toward abortion and demonstrates the kind of circuitous, vague, deceptive language and reasoning that Roth parodies and carries to illogical conclusion throughout the book. The first section, "Tricky Comforts a Troubled Citizen," introduces Dixon's stance on abortion, his opportunism as a politician, his legalistic obfuscation, and his obsession with the metaphor "Life is a game"—by which he most often means the good old boy, good old American games of football and baseball.

Roth devotes most of this section to an exposure of the incongruity between Dixon's so-called reverence for the life of the unborn and his total disregard for the lives of the hundreds of Vietnamese civilians killed at My Lai under the direction of the American Lieutenant Calley.[2] The absurdity of his position begins to become apparent when he is forced by an unrelenting citizen to admit that the killing of pregnant women at My Lai might be considered immoral because their deaths resulted in the deaths of unborn children. Finally, Roth makes Dixon's argument look entirely ridiculous when the citizen engages him in a debate over whether Calley was committing "abortion on demand" (to which Dixon is adamantly opposed) when he murdered women whom he knew to be pregnant. But true to his name, Tricky withdraws from the debate by reminding his opponent that since they are only supposing there to have been a pregnant woman among those killed, the discussion is "totally academic."

"Tricky Holds a Press Conference" further exposes Dixon's linguistic perversions by introducing his most dishonest and comical rhetorical technique—his insistence that he wants to make everything "most perfectly clear" when, in fact, he is using language to make things "perfectly unclear." In this context, Dixon identifies his defense of the unborn with Martin Luther King's fight for black rights and with the late Robert F. Charisma's (Kennedy's) support of the rights of Puerto Ricans and Chicanos. Recalling that King and Charisma were assassinated and made martyrs for advocating freedom and civil rights for deprived groups, Dixon assures his enemies that he will not be made to give up his struggle for the rights of the "disadvantaged" unborn. Realizing that this constituency lacks representation, and carried away with his own rhetoric, Dixon even proposes to extend the right to vote to the unborn and makes a plea to the press in his usual senseless jargon: "But what about Prenatal Power? Don't they have rights too, membranes though they be? I for one think they do, and I intend to fight for them."

Roth never misses an opportunity to accentuate the slips in grammar and logic that characterize Dixon's way of speaking, and at one point he has the President become so enthralled with his own argument that he promises to have everybody become "unborn." Concluding his press conference with a speech that recalls Martin Luther King's "I have a dream" address, he says: "My only hope is that whatever I am able to accomplish in their behalf while I hold this office will someday contribute to a world in which *everybody*, regardless of race, creed, or color, will be unborn. I guess if I have a dream, that is it."

In the first two chapters, Roth accentuates Dixon's abuse of language and logic; in the third, he suggests that such abuses imply a psychopathology of the politically ambitious. The scene that begins the section "Tricky Has Another Crisis; or, the Skull Session" has the flavor of stage directions in a play. Dixon has donned his football uniform from Prissier College and steals down to the "blast-proof underground locker room," where it is his habit to run plays before a mirror when he needs to quash his sense of personal fear. The dialogue begins only after it is apparent that because his attempts to "work out" his current problems are not succeeding, Dixon has called a "skull session," a secret meeting of his advisors. All of them appear dressed in football uniforms and ready to plan a "game strategy." Actually, they have met to assess a domestic crisis in which the Boy Scouts are demonstrating in Washington because Dixon's support of the unborn implies that he advocates sexual intercourse. Since everyone naturally maintains that sexual intercourse is immoral and un-American, Dixon considers announcing that he is a homosexual until one of his advisors informs him that homosexuals also "commit" sexual intercourse.

Dixon, knowing full well that he had really said nothing in his "unborn speech," cannot understand the cause of all the furor: "What did I say? Let's look at the record. I said *nothing! Absolutely nothing!* I came out for 'the rights of the unborn.' I mean if ever there was a line of hokum, that was it." Nevertheless, the

Boy Scouts of America are on television screaming
that "Trick E. Dixon favors sexual intercourse. Favors
fornication—between people!"

The chapter becomes an extravagant parody of
the way in which policy decisions are made and the
political opportunism and irrationality that motivate
them. Finally Dixon's team of advisors decides that it
has found a scapegoat for the Boy Scout scandal in
Curt Flood, the black baseball player who tried to
alter his major-league contract and ended up leaving
the country for Copenhagen. The President and his
sycophants decide to use the Flood case to end the
Boy Scout crisis, even if it means invading Denmark.
Apparently, for Dixon, the extent to which the end
justifies the means is limitless, and so is the peculiarity
of the means. Political expediency is the name of the
game, and no plan is too unscrupulous to be justified.
Dixon's parting words to his advisors demonstrate his
"ball-field" view of politics and his facility for por-
traying the ignoble in noble terms:

I will remain in uniform, helmet and all, and with the aid
of the ballots you have cast here in this free election, I
will hammer out, in the lonely vigil of the night, the conspiracy that seems to me most beneficial to my career. I
only hope and pray that I am equal to the task. Good
night, gentlemen, and thank you.

In order to put the Curt Flood strategy into effect, Dixon has to send troops to Denmark; and this
calls for an address to the American people ("The
Famous 'Something is Rotten in the State of Denmark'
Speech") in which he links the invasion of the "sov-
ereign state of Denmark" with that country's harbor-
ing Curt Flood and lays the blame for the Boy Scout
fiasco on Flood, a fugitive from justice.

Roth intends the portion of the speech in which
Dixon euphemistically refers to the invasion of Den-

mark as a "liberation" as a parody of the American government's way of describing its involvement in Vietnam. With his characteristically circuitous logic, the President maintains that American troops have liberated Elsinore from the "yoke of foreign domination," thus wrenching this historic site from the Danes and restoring it to the English-speaking peoples of the world. Further, Dixon's attack on the pro-pornography government in Copenhagen becomes a comment on the American attack on the pro-communist government in Vietnam. He indicates that despite his reluctance to interfere in the internal affairs of another country, the pro-pornography government has so brainwashed the Danish people that the DAR (Danish Anti-Pornography Resistance) received no votes in a "so-called free election." Consequently, America may have no choice but to use force in deposing the elected government of Copenhagen and installing a "government that will respond to reason instead of force."

With calculated irony, Roth has Dixon assassinated in the next-to-last chapter instead of the concluding chapter because in death, as in life, the President is determined to make a "comeback." For a time, however, Dixon's rhetoric is stilled and the focus shifts to the linguistic eccentricities of Vice President What's-his-name, who speaks in alliteration, and to the media "hype" that surrounds events of national importance. Roth has made apparent in other contexts his contempt for the mediocrity of both television and newspaper reporting, and here the ineptness of the media—and their hunger for every titillating morsel of specious information—catches the brunt of his satire. Reporters are stationed in all the major cities to relate, in somber tones, that particular city's reaction to the tragic news of the President's death—the details of which unfold slowly.

Dixon's habit of associating himself with political martyrs becomes a self-fulfilling prophecy when he is murdered by someone who has enticed him into a fluid-filled baggie, in which he drowns in the fetal position. His body is found in the delivery room of a hospital. Roth never misses a chance at irony, and here it is particularly apt: Dixon in death is united with the unborn, to whose welfare he has been so devoted. Finally, it is established that Dixon was drowned by "some lone nut" opposed to the rights of the unborn; and, at last, he has joined those who died for a cause. He becomes a "martyr to the unborn the world round." Yet unlike the thousands who attended the funeral of the other martyrs—Martin Luther King and Robert Charisma—the mob that comes to Dixon's funeral does not consist of respectful mourners filled with grief. Rather, as one of the news commentators says, these people "cometh" in guilt—to confess to the murder of the President. The implication seems to be that all people of good will wish they had had the good sense to try and rid the country of such fraudulent leadership. As one young mother confessing on television to Dixon's murder says: "Imagine it—my little girl is going to grow up in a world where she'll never have to hear anybody say he's going to make something perfectly clear ever again."

Tricky, however, is a hard man to keep down; and the book ends with "On the Comeback Trail," in which he addresses his "fellow Fallen" in hell. He is the challenger in this "diabolical" political campaign; his opponent is Satan, who he thinks has failed to use his capacity for evil and distortion to its fullest. Dixon himself is still attempting to "make one thing perfectly clear" as he tells the denizens of hell that what they need is a new administration, one with "new horns, new half-truths, new horrors and new hypocrisies." As always, he ends his appeal with a promise:

And let there be no mistake about it: if I am elected
Devil, I intend to see Evil triumph in the end; I intend to
see that our children, and our children's children, need
never know the terrible scourge of Righteousness and
Peace.

Given the scathing nature of the satire in *Our
Gang,* the book has naturally raised some essential
questions about the anticipated consequences of so
virulent an attack on a political figure. In an interview
with Alan Lelchuk, Roth defends himself against the
inevitable accusation that his satire is incendiary by
insisting upon the essential difference between words
and deeds. He emphasizes that, obviously, deeds are
the more deadly of the two by pointing out that
"more people are killed in this country every year by
bullets than by satires." When Lelchuk infers that the
assassination chapter could be construed by readers
as advocating the murder of President Nixon and
wonders what other purpose Roth had in writing it,
Roth points out first that the ludicrous manner in
which Dixon is murdered—stuffed in a baggy—ought
to indicate that his death is "just satiric retribution,
parodic justice." He then maintains that this chapter
ridicules primarily the discrepancy between government and media pieties and the "unpleasant truth"
and mocks the "platitudinous mentality of the media"
as much as anything else. Roth makes it clear that his
satire is not aimed exclusively at one man or one
group but at all—citizens, the press, presidents, presidential advisors—who deliberately use language to fal-
sify meaning. A final comment emphasizes the extent
to which Roth connects media distortion of reality
with governmental distortion:

That chapter entitled "The Assassination of Tricky" is
largely at the expense of network blindness. The implication is that the mass media are purveyors of the Official

Version of Reality and, for all their so-called criticism of
the government, can be counted on, when the chips are
down, to cloud the issue and miss the point.

Lastly, the chapter is concerned with the fine art of
government lying, but then so is the entire book.

The Great American Novel

Our Gang takes as its subject the American "game" of
politics and exposes the ways in which the unscrupulous pervert and use American ideals to accomplish
their own corrupt goals. *The Great American Novel,*
Roth's most ambitious and most direct exposé of the
failed American dream, ostensibly takes as its subject
the American game of baseball. Published two years
after the political satire, this novel replaces what Roth
calls the "satiric bull's eye" of *Our Gang* with a "good-
sized imaginary world" more loosely connected to the
actual than *Our Gang*. In style and form, it is more
wildly experimental than any of Roth's other books;
and the critical response to Roth's experimentation,
although varied as usual, has generally been less positive than usual.

The harshest reactions to the book were from writers like Webster Schott of the *Washington Post Book
World,* who called it a "great American bore that's
impossible not to put down shortly after you pick it
up." [3] A few considered the book a brilliant satire in
which the game of baseball parallels the game of
American life. According to Christopher Lehmann-
Haupt, it is a "relaxing masterpiece of fantasy." [4] Most
of the reviewers, however, were mixed in their reactions—recognizing the grandeur of Roth's attempt
and the validity of his satire but lamenting the book's
diffuseness and failure to entertain. William H. Gass
is typical in his admiration of Roth's skill at mimicking

the absurdity of the "Americanized" game of baseball, with its devotion to "Gun, God, and Flag" and its "shabby morality of Fair Play," its all-consuming greed. Gass, like others, also sees Roth using baseball as a metaphor for a way of life that has become obsessively and destructively competitive. Finally, however, he concludes that Roth's antics compromise the purpose of the novel and leave the readers expecting a resolution that they do not get.[5] Thomas R. Edwards is more precise about what detracts from the novel when he says that "Roth's determination to get in every joke he can think of about our past and present follies—patriotic paranoia, racism, sexual infantilism, the vulgarity of the media—finally is exhausting and self-defeating." [6]

In an essay that appeared in *Contemporary Literature* in 1976, Ben Siegel links the distorted nature of American life and values to the tendency of many recent writers to use farce and slapstick in emphasizing the "thinness of line between dream and reality, fantasy and fact, comedy and pathos." His perspective corresponds to Roth's assessment of the contemporary writer's dilemma—the difficulty of making reality credible in fiction—presented in "Writing American Fiction." Siegel sees Roth attacking society's "most deeply embedded pieties and hypocrisies, enthusiasms and lunacies; his special targets are America's hyper-patriots and racists, her adolescent sexists and media vulgarians." He thinks that baseball is a particularly apt vehicle for such satire because its "public pose" of winning by fair play provides an obvious symbol for American life. Whatever the vehicle, however, the object of Roth's attack is consistently the "disparity in American life between appearance and reality, between professed idealism or good will and an underlying self-seeking grossness or vulgarity." [7]

The farcical, fantastical *Great American Novel*
begins with a prologue and a self-introduction by the
first-person narrator, one Word Smith, whose open-
ing statement is "Call me Smitty." He is an ancient
sportswriter and fan of the now-defunct Patriot League
of baseball, which had at one time been ranked with
the American and National leagues. Although Smitty
is now confined to Valhalla, a home for the aged and
very infirm, he is determined to write the "Great
American Novel" that will restore the reputation and
heritage of the suppressed Patriot League and the
Ruppert Mundys—both of which became so corrupt
and ridiculous that fans and officials alike joined in a
conspiracy to erase them from the national record
and memory.

Throughout the story, but especially in his introduction to himself and his task, Smitty alludes to
almost all the possible contenders for the title of "Great
American Novelist," poking fun at the writers and
their claims and at a literary establishment that has
itself been corrupted by the American notion of success. The top contender for the "prize" of "best creator
of the great American myth" seems to be Herman
Melville, but Nathaniel Hawthorne's and Mark
Twain's [8] credentials are also examined and their
styles parodied. And there is an extended comment
on the macho-competitiveness of Ernest Hemingway,
who denigrates all other writers as well as the entire
literary and scholastic establishment in his ongoing
attempt to assure himself that *he* really is the greatest
American novelist.

Smitty's introductory allusions to literary figures
and their works not only serve to establish the context of his novel and his kinship with his literary
precursors, they also give him an opportunity to define
himself and his work through comparisons with them.
His analysis of the predicament of the slave Jim in

The Adventures of Huckleberry Finn, for example, while giving him a chance to condemn the suppression of the members of the Patriot League, also reveals a connection between the picaresque mode of an American classic and the structure of his own book. Making observations about *Moby Dick* allows him to compare himself to Ishmael—one who survived the "wreck to tell the tale"; and his examination of Hawthorne's *Scarlet Letter* leads him to distinguish his own novel from Hawthorne's by claiming for it an authenticity that his predecessor's tale lacked. Even Chaucer's *Canterbury Tales,*[9] although not in the running for the designation of "Great American Novel," figures in Smitty's introduction as a way to suggest his own pilgrimage and that of the Mundys. And at times, through Smitty's blend of literary impression and baseball statistics, Roth allows the reader a glimpse of his own pilgrimage as a writer. At one point, Smitty, sounding very much like Roth defending his own vision of the truth, tells his critics:

Well, fans, I suppose there are those who called Geoffrey Chaucer (*and* William Shakespeare, with whom I share initials) a crazy coot, and immoral, and so on down the line. Tell them what they do not wish to hear, tell them that they have got it wrong, and the first thing out of their mouths, "You're off your nut!" Understanding this as I do should make me calm and philosophical, I know. Wise, sagacious, and so forth. Only it doesn't work that way.

Since his earliest works, Roth has been accused of writing "immoral" fiction; and as he began to satirize facets of the American experience more obviously, he has been in the position of "telling them what they do not wish to hear." His love-hate relationship with contemporary American society has been reciprocated by a fair proportion of that society. As many of his remarks indicate, throughout the course of his career Roth has become increasingly aware of his readers' propensity for rejecting any version of reality that contradicts their own. Yet understanding this, as Smitty says, does not necessarily make him philosophical or calm.

Smitty, the "old truth-teller," concludes his "Prologue" with a prophecy that the obliteration of the Patriot League is merely a forerunner of the destruction of the planet itself: "The cushy long-term lease has just about run out on this Los Angeles of a franchise called Earth—and yes. . . . you too will be out on your dispossessed ass, Mr. and Mrs. Roaring Success." Here is the pervasive theme throughout Roth's satire: the self-destructiveness of the success madness inherent in the philosophy of Americanism. Smitty's story, *The Great American Novel,* becomes an exemplum of this theme. But from Smitty's perspective, the purpose of his tale is to restore the Patriot League (the Port Ruppert Mundys, Tri-City Tycoons, Tri-City Greenbacks, Asylum Keepers, Kakoola Reapers, Aceldema Butchers, Independence Blues, and Terra Incognita Rustlers) to its rightful place in the history of baseball.

His chronicle begins in the summer of 1943, when World War II conspires with the greed and irresponsibility of the team's owners to deprive the Ruppert Mundys of their playing field and force them to go on the road for a year. The journey is characterized by increasing misfortunes and a record of 31 and 123 by a team that the draft has reduced to a grotesque collection of cripples, misfits, and psychopaths. An important element in this portion of the story is the quarrel between Gil Gamesh, the last of the Mundy heroes, and the respected umpire, Mike Masterson. An altercation between the two ends with the maiming of the umpire and the banishment of Gil, who

eventually returns to America as a spy after years of
Communist training. Upon his return, Gamesh convinces the league commissioner, General Douglas D.
Oakhart, that Reds are infiltrating the league; but at
the same time, he is inciting the team to rebel against
the oppressions of capitalism. Gamesh's double ploy
works and stirs the team to victory until his duplicity
is discovered by the team's best player and only
innocent, Roland Agni. Agni is then mysteriously murdered and Gamesh wounded by the irate Masterson,
who has returned at last for his revenge.

Finally, the team is destroyed and everyone involved subjected to a congressional investigation.
Within this bare plot structure, however, the incidents
and intricacies multiply *ad infinitum:* Mike Masterson's daughter is kidnapped; the Mundys' manager,
Ulysses S. Fairsmith, goes to Japan and Africa with
the intention of converting the heathen to baseball;
Roland Agni collaborates with a Jewish child genius
to feed the Mundys Jewish Wheaties; Angela Whittling Trust, owner of the Tri-City Tycoons, engages
in numerous sexual exploits. All these narrative incidents take place within the framework of Roth's usual
line of satire, wherein he attacks those aspects of
American life which he finds most abhorrent—or sometimes merely ridiculous.

Characteristically, Roth makes the use and abuse
of language a primary target for his satire, and several
versions of the rhetoric of delusion come in for lengthy
parody. Among the most extravagant and skillful of
these renditions is Fairsmith's application of religion
and patriotism to the Great American way of winning.
"For what is a ball park," he asks rhetorically, "but
that place wherein Americans may gather to worship
the beauty of God's earth, the skill and strength of His
children, and the holiness of His commandment to
order and obedience." This particular tirade is in re-

sponse to the threat of having to break with tradition by playing baseball under electric lights—contrary to the will of God. Fairsmith thinks it equally ungodly to broadcast a baseball game "live." He maintains that "You might as well put an announcer up in the woods in October and have him do a 'live' broadcast of the fall, as describe a baseball game on the radio." Ultimately, Fairsmith's rhetoric of conservatism lumps together everything traditional; customary attitudes and practices in religion, baseball, patriotism, government, and family life become interchangeable and are used to validate one another. Out of this perspective, he utters the peculiar truth that to his way of thinking, "Baseball is this country's religion."

The introduction of the Patriot League's first midget, Bob Yamm, gives Roth an opportunity to parody simultaneously the rhetoric of human rights and the rhetoric of media exploitation. Yamm delivers several long speeches on his behalf in which he maintains that he speaks not only for himself "but for all midgets everywhere"; and as the spokesman for this oppressed group, he insists on his rights "as an American and a human being" and opposes the "conspiracy" to prevent people of his stature from playing baseball. Both Yamm's and Fairsmith's uses of the rhetoric of delusion demonstrate the dishonest manipulation of language that Roth thinks so characteristic of American public life.

Ironically, Fairsmith's rhetoric of conservatism and Yamm's rhetoric of civil rights sound very much alike. Working from opposite perspectives, the conservative and the liberal, each invokes self-righteous, self-evident platitudes on behalf of his opinions, and each avoids any systematic adherence to logic. Roth does not limit his satire of language distortion to the "rhetoricians" Fairsmith and Yamm, however, for he closely associates Yamm's civil-rights stand and his use of language to delude with the sugary, sentimentalized, dishonest reaction of the media and the public to him. With all the pretensions to profundity that characterized the purveyors of news and public opinion in *Our Gang,* the reporters herald Yamm as a "midget to be proud of." One columnist solemnly asks, "Why are our brave boys fighting and dying in far-off lands, if not so that the Bob Yamm's of this world can hold high their heads, midgets though they may be?" Yamm becomes a media sensation—a *cause*—and the entire fickle nation takes him and all midgets "to its heart."

Gil Gamesh's double-dealing with the Communists and the Americans provides Roth another means of parodying a particular brand of rhetoric—this time the language that he associates with the conflict between Communism and American patriotism. Mrs. Whittling Trust's description of the activities of the Communist Party in baseball has all the earmarks of the "redbaiting" of the McCarthy era (a time in American history that Roth finds particularly offensive).[10] Like the McCarthyites, Mrs. Whittling Trust accuses almost everybody of being involved in a Communist conspiracy to destroy the free enterprise system—and baseball. She insists that the enemies of America are "going to turn the people, not only against the national game, but simultaneously against the profit system itself." In its turn, Gamesh's description of his collaboration with the Communist effort to infiltrate the country and destroy baseball supports her position and, finally, mocks the language of Communism in America.

In the end, however, Gamesh's notion of American competition and baseball sounds as fanatical as his version of Communism. He tells how he wandered the "length and breadth" of this land and of Russia, growing more and more homesick for American baseball. But his most outlandish use of the language comes in that combination of the rhetoric of American competition and the rhetoric of Communist propaganda (reflecting his role as double agent) with which he attempts to inspire the Mundys to win a few more games:

You are scum because you do not hate your oppressors. You are slaves and fools and jellyfish because you do not loathe your enemies. . . . Just think of all the things you haven't got that other people have. Shall I name a few just to get you going? . . . Don't you *understand,* boys? It isn't *fair!* It isn't *just!* It isn't *right!* . . . Mundys, it isn't *God* that put you on the road! It isn't *fate,* and it isn't nothing, either. It is your *fellow man!* Who made you scapegoats, Mundys? The United States government and the Brothers M.! The country whose flag you salute, the owners whose names you bear! That's who joined forces to rob you of honor and dignity and home! The state and the owners! Your country and your bosses!

Through such double-talk diatribes as these, he inspires the Mundys for a while.

In addition to satirizing rhetoric, baseball, American naiveté, greed, competition, and politics, Roth also takes passing shots at racism and sexism, and his familiar targets—the American nuclear family and the relationship between the sexes. To emphasize the overprotective and destructive relationships between "Mommies" and "Daddies" and their children, he constructs several scenes in which the local "Moms" adopt the Mundys on "Ladies Day" after the Mundys' loss to the Kakoola Reapers. The Mundy Moms take over their surrogate children and turn the players into dependent babies—bathing them, spoon-feeding them, and tucking them into bed. Roth's target here is "Super-Momism" and the rhetoric that produces and validates forever-dominating mothers. "Dadism" and the everlasting childishness it produces receive similar treatment in the scenes between Frank Maxuma (the greedy owner of the Kakoola Reapers) and his daughters. Infantilism, overprotective parents, and childish dependencies have been subjects of Roth's in other, less fantastical books, but there the emphasis was on the psychological manifestations of these conditions. In this book, the manifestation is external and in caricature as Roth exaggerates the maladies inherent in American families.

In an essay written shortly after the publication of *The Great American Novel*, Roth describes the book as an expression of a comic, extravagant quality that had previously been suppressed—at least to some extent—in his fiction. Here, although Roth plays down the satiric nature of the book and insists that its major purpose is "comic inventiveness," he admits that the baseball metaphor serves mainly to dramatize the struggle between our national myth and the realities of American life. "Smitty's book," he says, "like those of his illustrious forebears, attempts to imagine a myth of an ailing America; my own is to some extent an attempt to imagine a book about imagining that American myth." Later in the essay, Roth comments on the emphasis he had placed on "high seriousness" and moral responsibility in his earlier writings and indicates that books such as *The Great American Novel* and *Our Gang* express the other side of his literary nature—the one he inherited from influences like the Jewish comic Henny Youngman—as opposed to those which go back to his literary mentors, Henry James and Flaubert. Roth's comments suggest that he sees this book as an important step in the development of his art, a kind of liberation from the burden of having to view writing as a "priestly" pursuit. He says:

To sum up: the comic recklessness that I've identified with my old mentor, Jake the Snake, the indecent candy-store owner, apparently could not develop to its fullest until the *subject* of restraints and taboos had been dramatized in a series of increasingly pointed fictions that revealed the possible consequences of banging your head against your own wall.

While Roth locates the impetus for risking the "recklessness" of *The Great American Novel* in a nonliterary tradition, Bernard Rodgers, a recent commentator on Roth's work, sees the book as stemming almost altogether from the humor and traditions of the American Southwest and points out the similarities between it and that tradition. Both derive from the vernacular humor of masculine pastimes; both rely heavily on the humor of physical discomfort, exaggeration, and popular myth. Rodgers also connects the structure of the story (the frame tale, or the tale within a tale) with Old Southwest humor. He summarizes his interpretation with a significant observation about the increasingly fantastical nature of the book: "The same tall-tale pattern is repeated again and again in each of the book's chapters; but each time the line between reality and fantasy becomes more difficult to discern, and the casual reader is increasingly hard put to keep track of just where each tale crosses the line." [11] Thus, in this book that Roth says incorporates a "good-sized imaginary world," the depiction of America becomes more and more fantastic and mythic—an image of America rather than a portrait. *The Great American Novel* is Roth's ultimate indictment of a big dream gone awry in a big way.

"On the Air"

In 1970, between the publication of *Portnoy's Complaint* and *Our Gang*, a short story of Roth's called "On the Air" [12] appeared in the *New American Re-*

view. A masterpiece of reality confusion and bizarre humor, the story is linked both thematically and stylistically to *Our Gang* and *The Great American Novel*. Like the latter, it has a simple plot based on a pilgrimage, or a picaresque journey, made complex by the multiplication of unbelievably strange events. The hero is one Milton Lippman, an unsuccessful shoe salesman with a penchant for "show biz." A man who believes in "the power of the radio," Lippman becomes incensed by a gentile radio commentator who calls himself the "Answer Man" and purports to know the answer to all the questions his listeners ask him. Thinking that there ought to be a program "with a Jew on it giving out the answers," Lippman, a some-time talent scout, comes up with the idea of putting Einstein on the air as the Jewish (and thus authentic) Answer Man to prove the old adage that Jews are smarter than *goyim*—and, of course, to promote his own "career" as a talent agent. After three letters to Einstein, all unanswered, he decides to take his family on a trip (one day from New York to Prince-ton) to meet Einstein and discuss the matter—or at least to give his son a glimpse of Einstein's house and maybe of Einstein himself.

Within this frame, the story, like *The Great American Novel*, deals mainly with conflicting ver-sions of reality and the relationship between fantasy and reality, truth and fiction, life and art. One of the central conflicts emphasizes the difference between "Jewish truth" and "gentile truth." Each kind regards the other as inferior and wrong—even crazy. What bothers Lippman most is that the Answer Man is spreading gentile truth (*"goyische* bullshit") as if it were *the* truth. He thinks that a Jew such as Einstein, "THE GENIUS OF ALL TIME," probably *really* knows the truth. But then the real truth is relative, as the allusions to Einstein's theory of relativity suggest.

In fact, nothing could be more relative than the Answer's Man's answers, which actually are nonanswers —mere open-ended commentary that leaves room for almost any interpretation.

In the first letter to Einstein, Lippman tells of his discovery of the "Famous Brothers" and introduces the fantastic nature of reality. The "Brothers" are black shoeshine boys who not only are not performers and not famous, they are not even brothers. Furthermore, by no stretch of the imagination is Lippman really a talent scout. Soon it becomes clear that the definition of reality and the relationship of reality to art (with show business as the exemplar of art) are central to the meaning of the story. Maintaining that "hearing is believing," Lippman urges Einstein to go on the radio so that all the doubting Thomases will believe that he is more than a name and is truly the "smartest person alive." In Lippman's mind, only art can validate reality.

As Lippman undertakes his pilgrimage to Einstein's house, he becomes involved in several incidents that play ironically on the maxim that "seeing is believing." These episodes, to which Roth gives such titles as "Duffy's Tavern," "Gangbusters," and "The Lone Ranger," recall the radio shows of the 1930s and 1940s. In "Duffy's Tavern," Lippman and his wife and timid little son stop at an ice cream parlor that turns out to be a surrealistic gentile bar-bowling alley. In many ways, the "Tavern" confirms the Lippmans' worst suspicions about Gentiles. The goyim do inhabit dark places for the purposes of consuming alcohol, a habit that the Lippmans find odd, decadent, and pointless. In this foreign environment, however, Milton notices a "strangeness beyond the ordinary strangeness." The bar is peculiarly decorated with a variety of artifacts that suggest violence; and the bartender, a black man wearing the cotton gloves of a garbage collector, is dressed like Joe Louis in the picture that hangs on the wall behind him.

At first glimpse, Lippman wonders whether he is hallucinating or imagining things; but immediately he recalls the main lesson that life has taught him: "what you can imagine could also be so." What could be stranger, he thinks, than real-life events and people like Hitler—"that little nut over in Germany thundering and howling at those millions of German people, and them saluting and cheering back. . . . Hitler! What an *idea!*" And for sheer ridiculousness, what about leaders with the unlikely looks of Mussolini or the Roosevelts, or the Pope, a man wearing a dress and "telling them, 'Dominoes chess checkers' " and making people believe they are going to live forever. Lippman concludes, "Now, if that is no hallucination, then what is?" The point, of course, is that all of this is reality that from a certain perspective appears to be as incredible as an illusion; consequently, for Lippman, illusions can be as credible as reality.

With this kind of perspective, Lippman views the real world as being full of "acts." Everywhere he looks, there is "entertainment material galore." Lippman's view of life suggests the predicament of the artist, whose job is to represent a world that is already "fictionalized." When Lippman's wife reprimands him for seeing entertainment in things that are "serious," he defends himself with words that recall Roth's defense of the writer who tries to depict modern life in all its realistic absurdity. Lippman protests to his wife:

"But I am not ashamed! I will not be ashamed! I am a talent scout! I have to have an eye for the gimmick, for the strange! People don't notice the unusual things that happen in life until somebody that does comes along and points them out. And that is all I do, and is nothing I will 'be ashamed of.' A talent scout is only a person who happens to see what the other person doesn't—he doesn't make these things happen, *he only points them out!*"

She didn't understand. It wasn't as though *he* had put the Pope in a dress. It wasn't as though *he* had given Mrs. Roosevelt those teeth. Lippman was only pointing them out, that they were *there*. "God," he announced to his wife, "God is the Greatest Talent Scout of Us All!"

Here Lippman's words are reminiscent of Roth's as he laments the predicament of the contemporary American writer whose task is to make fiction out of events already too strange to be believed in "Writing American Fiction." Both Lippman and Roth defend themselves against the accusation that they are responsible for a world they only try to depict, and they imply that a reality such as the present one can be presented only as satire or fantasy. For Lippman (and for Roth) the way to master an absurd reality is to capture it in all its absurdity. In "On the Air," Roth tries to solve the modern writer's dilemma by using what might be called "satirical fantasy" to portray the surrealism of the "real" world.

From the "Duffy's Tavern" section, the story spirals further and further into a realm where the demarcation between fact and fantasy is obscure and the satire is carried out through a constellation of absurd symbolism. There is, for example, "Scoop," the demented soda jerk at Howard Johnson's, who has an ice cream scoop for a hand, and "Pop Scully," the manager of the establishment, who looks like a newspaper man and gives Lippman's son newspaper-flavored ice cream, which poisons him. Roth, of course, constructs this bit of detail to attack his old enemy, the press. There is a testicle-weighing contest between Lippman, an unwilling participant, and a violent police chief, a parody of radio and television lawmen, through which Roth satirizes the contemporary American image of masculinity—particularly the type of maleness important to gentile men. There is a shootout in which a bullet ricochets off Lippman's nose and kills the police chief, giving rise to a bystander's comment that Lippman "Jewed him right down—in cold blood." The story concludes with an announcer's voice reminding the listening audience to "tune in to this same wavelength tomorrow" for more in the adventures of Milton Lippman. Finally, the reader realizes that it has all been a show within a show, in much the same way that Word Smith's novel is within a novel. And somewhere out there beyond the "wavelengths" is the absurd "reality" that has fostered these absurd "illusions."

For Roth, that "reality" is found in the American experience. He has said that it is naive to expect satire to effect a change in the world, to serve an "ameliorative function." Writing satire, he suggests, is a literary rather than a political or social act. Satire is, however, a way to make an imaginative assault upon social and political acts; and from that perspective, Roth has, in such playful works as *Our Gang, The Great American Novel,* and "On the Air," made a deadly serious attack upon the distortions and perversions inherent in the American myth.

4

○○○

Philip Roth:
After Eleven Books

During the course of what has become a twenty-year writing career, Philip Roth has assiduously examined the double edge of his own fame—the high praise and the bitter criticism that have characterized reactions to his work. When he quotes Rilke, who wrote that "fame is no more than the quintessence of all the misunderstandings collecting around a new name," Roth reveals the extent to which he regards misunderstanding as the basis of much of his notoriety as a writer. Roth was in his twenties when he became a "new name" to the reading public. For some, the name was associated with well-wrought stories that explored a Jewish character's crisis of identity; for others, it was associated with a betrayal of Jewish religion and culture. Such an early adverse reaction from, primarily, members of the Jewish community obviously came as a shock to Roth, a young devotee of the idea of fiction as a "religious calling." Stories such as "Epstein" and "Defender of the Faith" drew considerable fire for what some considered to be a negative portrayal of the Jews, and Roth unexpectedly found himself accused of treachery and immorality and his work indicted for fostering anti-Semitism. Almost simultaneously, those same stories, collected and published in the volume *Goodbye, Columbus*, were being acclaimed and Roth hailed as one of the "most forcefully

intelligent and serious" contemporary writers. Nevertheless, the accusations struck a nerve, and Roth has repeatedly defended himself against the charges of racial
disloyalty and sexual indiscretion that started with the
publication of *Goodbye, Columbus* and culminated in
the uproar surrounding *Portnoy's Complaint.*

From the beginning, Roth has insisted that the
purpose of literature is to expand "moral consciousness" rather than reflect desired or acceptable behavior and that the fictionalist's job is to present human (not just Jewish) possibility. As recently as *The
Ghost Writer,* he summarizes his position in the characterization of Amy-Anne Frank, who insists that if
she is to be exceptional, it will be because of what she
has made of herself—not because of Auschwitz and
Belsen.

Portnoy's Complaint made Roth rich, made him
famous, and to some, made him the "bad boy" of contemporary American fiction. In writing about his and
Portnoy's fame, Roth uses the same kind of terminology
that he does when reflecting on the early recognition
Goodbye, Columbus brought him. Again he recalls
his "priestly literary education," the "moral seriousness" with which he was taught to regard fiction writing, and the surprising turn of events by which fame
came to him as scandal rather than honor. Significantly, he focuses on the moral seriousness of a book
that depicts an "overwhelming obsession" with the
conscience in conflict with itself. Portnoy "is obscene,"
according to Roth, "because he wants to be saved." It
is just this strange connection between obscenity and
salvation that lies at the center of the book. Roth insists here as elsewhere on the revealing link between
the psychological reality of the individual and the
way that reality is verbalized.

In addition to being the focal point of considerable criticism from the Jewish community, Roth's work

has often been attacked by feminist writers, who regard his vivid portrayal of disruptive women as evidence of antifeminism. Roth's heroines are often more powerful and more destructive than his men, and this has led to the view that his novels are designed to castigate women in general.

Mary Allen's conclusions in her chapter on *When She Was Good* in *The Necessary Blankness: Women in Major American Fiction of the Sixties* are characteristic. She indicates that in Roth's "creation of heroines, he projects his enormous rage and disappointment with womankind, writing with power and conviction, but as a man who rails at the world because he has never found in it a woman who is both strong and good." [1] In many ways, the feminist criticism of Roth has been as one-sided as much of the Jewish criticism. It overlooks the fact that it is primarily through women that the weaknesses of men are revealed and that neither Roth's men nor his women are both "strong and good." And among contemporary male writers, it is Roth, more than anyone else, who recognizes (as he makes plain through Tarnopol in *My Life as a Man*) that male inviolability is a myth and that female "toughness" is a technique for survival. For Roth, men and women are caught together in a trap of social conditioning that makes it impossible for either sex to escape the interchangeable roles of victim and victimizer.

After eleven books, all of which mingle the serious, the comic, and the satiric, Roth has shown himself to be an incisive observer of the American social and political scene. Clearly, his greatest accomplishments lie in his ability to probe the American consciousness and reveal its major conflicts—between the society and the individual, between men and women, between the need for security and the desire for adventure, between the myth of American culture and

the reality. Roth is among those writers to whom
Leslie Fiedler refers when he notes that American
Jewish writers have played a key role in presenting
images of contemporary American life.[2]

As with other recent novelists, Roth's vision is
more often particular than cosmic; or, to put it more
accurately, Roth's vision requires that he move from
the specific to the universal, detailing the psychological and sociological peculiarities of life in twentieth-
century America and linking them ultimately to the
universal issues of human identity, the passing of
time, and the relationship between good and evil.
When She Was Good, "Eli, the Fanatic," *Portnoy's
Complaint*, and all the "professor" stories delineate
the predicament of the individual engaged in a life
and death struggle with all the internal and external
forces of control, while the political books attack specific political abuses in the light of the more comprehensive problems of authority and power. Roth portrays a secularized society that takes its religion where
it can—in baseball, in patriotism, in ethnic chauvinism,
in human relationships—and points to the universali-
ties of the human condition that lie beneath the secular facade.

Within the literary establishment, Roth is most
widely acclaimed—and deservedly—for his mastery
of vernacular language. More accurately than any
other living writer, he has been able to capture the
cadences of everyday speech and to suggest through
dialogue the meaning of everyday events. Roth began
in *Goodbye, Columbus* and the short stories to render
the character of urban Jewish culture and later joined
Jewish life and language to that of the academic
world. In *When She Was Good*, he left the milieu
with which he was most familiar and proved himself
equally skillful in projecting (and parodying) the
middle-class quality of the Protestant Midwest. In the

later books, he re-creates with clarity and sensitivity the rhetoric of radio, television, politics, and the mass movements of the 1960s. For Roth, the connection between language and meaning remains absolute, and no one has been more successful than he in dramatizing the significance of that connection.

Philip Roth, who began his writing career in the late 1950s and published his most recent book in 1979 at the age of forty-six, has lived through and chronicled a period of great change in American politics and mores. His work demonstrates those changes, and he has noted that *Portnoy's Complaint* and *The Great American Novel* reflect the "de-mythologizing" influence of the 1960s. Although much of Roth's strength as a novelist lies in his ability to mirror the fluctuating times in which he lives, he has from the beginning been concerned with a central cluster of themes—and a consistent method of presentation—to which he has remained faithful.

Notes

INTRODUCTION

1. Theodore Solotaroff, "The Journey of Philip Roth," *Atlantic* 223 (April 1969), 64–72.
2. R. Z. Sheppard, "The Novel: Very Warm for May," *Time*, 7 May 1973, p. 65.
3. Interview with Guinevera Nance in London on April 9, 1979.
4. Flannery O'Connor (1925–1964) was a southern writer whose stories demonstrated the plight of Christianity in the modern world through a combination of parody and exaggeration that has often been called grotesque.

1. GOOD GIRLS AND BOYS GONE BAD

1. Prufrock is the "indecisive modern man" of T. S. Eliot's famous poem "The Love Song of J. Alfred Prufrock" (1915).
2. In Arthur Miller's play *Death of a Salesman* (1949), the aging Willy Loman represents the failures of the American Dream.
3. Stanley Trachtenberg, "The Hero in Stasis," *Critique* 7 (Winter 1964/65), 5.
4. John N. McDaniel, *The Fiction of Philip Roth* (Haddonfield, N.J.: Haddonfield House, 1974), p. 76.
5. In Jonathan Swift's *Gulliver's Travels*, Gulliver's

second voyage takes him to Brobdingnag, a land oc-
cupied by creatures ten times the size of Europeans.

6. Bernard F. Rodgers, Jr., *Philip Roth* (Boston: Twayne Publishers, 1978), p. 22.

7. A "yeshivah" is a Jewish day school.

8. "Goyim" is a Yiddish word for non-Jews, often used disparagingly.

9. "*In medias res*" is Latin for "into the middle of things." It is chiefly used to refer to the classical literary or dramatic device whereby an author starts his narrative by plunging the reader into the middle of a sequence of events.

10. Henry James (1843–1916) is best known for his intricate style and restrained manner of storytelling.

11. In the April 9, 1979, interview with Guinevera Nance, Roth said that the word "good" is examined in most of his novels, that he attempts to find out what it is —what are the uses to which people put the idea of "good" and the uses to which it puts them. Roth said that even the "Nixon book" (*Our Gang*) comes out of that concern.

12. "Shiksa" or "shikse" is a Yiddish word for a non-Jewish girl, often used disparagingly.

13. Aristotle (384–322 B.C.), a Greek philosopher, maintains in his *Poetics* that one of the functions of the dramatist is to relate in his play what is possible according to the law of probability or necessity. Probability implies that what happens in a drama arises naturally and inevitably, by casual interrelation out of what precedes it.

14. "Oedipus complex" is a psychoanalytic term deriving from the Greek myth of Oedipus and implying the libidinal feelings of a child, usually male, for the parent of the opposite sex.

15. The French writer Gustave Flaubert (1821–1880), like Henry James, is one of Roth's models of the "novel of restraint." In *Madame Bovary*, Flaubert recounts the tragic story of a dissatisfied woman unable to adjust to the mediocrity of bourgeois life.

16. Franz Kafka (1883–1924) used comedic and absurd techniques to depict the serious and tragic in fiction.
17. Granville Hicks, "Literary Horizons," *Saturday Review*, 22 February 1969, pp. 38–39.
18. Marya Mannes, "A Dissent from Marya Mannes," *Saturday Review*, 22 February 1969, p. 39.
19. Thomas Mann (1875–1955), the Nobel Prize-winning German novelist, published *Death in Venice* in 1911. It portrays the moral collapse of a successful writer, brought about by an uncontrollable and humiliating passion for a boy.

2. A RAKE AMONG SCHOLARS, A SCHOLAR AMONG RAKES

1. George Gordon, Lord Byron (1788–1824) was a Romantic poet famous for his creation of the nonconforming "Byronic hero."
2. Richard Steele (1672–1729) was an English essayist, playwright, and journalist.
3. Theodore Solotaroff, "Fiction," *Esquire*, October 1972, pp. 82–84.
4. In Swift's *Gulliver's Travels* human beings are variously transformed. In Kafka's short story "The Metamorphosis" a man turns into a beetle. In "The Nose" by the Russian short-story writer Nikolai Gogol (1809–1852) the hero becomes a nose.
5. Aldous Huxley, *Point Counter Point* (New York: Harper & Row, 1965), pp. 301–2.
6. Virginia Woolf (1882–1941), like Flaubert and James, is one of Roth's models of restraint.
7. Mark Shechner, "Philip Roth," *Partisan Review* 41 (1974), 423.
8. Melvin Maddocks, "Make It New," *Time*, 10 June 1974, p. 92.
9. The American writer Henry Miller (1891–1980) and the Frenchman Louis-Ferdinand Céline (1894–1961) were novelists famous for the confessional, explicit nature of their fiction.

10.   Roth often depicts Helen in a way that suggests Helen of Troy, the beautiful troublemaker of Greek mythology.

11.   Anton Chekhov (1860–1904), the Russian short-story writer and dramatist, figures prominently in Roth's most recent books.

3. ROTH'S SATIRE: SHEER PLAYFULNESS AND DEADLY SERIOUSNESS

1.   George Orwell (1903–1950) was a British novelist and essayist, author of *Animal Farm* (1946) and *Nineteen Eighty-Four* (1949).

2.   The "My Lai incident" in the Vietnam war was a massacre of Vietnamese civilians by American soldiers. On March 16, 1968, a unit of the U.S. Army led by Lieutenant William L. Calley invaded a South Vietnamese hamlet and shot to death unarmed civilians, including women and children. Knowledge of the event did not reach the American public until autumn 1969.

3.   Webster Schott, "No Joy in Mudville," *Washington Post Book World,* 13 May 1973, p. 7.

4.   Christopher Lehmann-Haupt, "Philip Roth's Bathtub Novel," *New York Times,* 14 May 1973, p. 29.

5.   William Gass, "The Sporting News," *New York Review of Books,* 31 May 1973, p. 7.

6.   Thomas R. Edwards, *New York Times Book Review,* 6 May 1973, p. 27.

7.   Ben Siegel, "The Myths of Summer: Philip Roth's *The Great American Novel,*" *Contemporary Literature* 17 (1976), 171–90.

8.   Herman Melville published *Moby Dick* in 1851; Nathaniel Hawthorne published *The Scarlet Letter* in 1850; Mark Twain published *The Adventures of Huckleberry Finn* in 1884.

9.   Geoffrey Chaucer (ca. 1340–1400), a British writer, wrote the *Canterbury Tales,* a masterpiece of early

fiction that uses the devices of the journey and the tale within a tale.

10. During the 1950s Senator Joseph Raymond Mc-Carthy used his power as chairman of the Senate permanent investigations subcommittee to uncover persons suspected of Communist or subversive activities.

11. Bernard F. Rodgers, Jr., *Philip Roth* (Boston: Twayne Publishers, 1978), p. 118.

12. Philip Roth, "On the Air," *New American Review* 10 (1970), 7–49.

4. PHILIP ROTH: AFTER ELEVEN BOOKS

1. Mary Allen, "Philip Roth: When She Was Good She Was Horrid," in *The Necessary Blankness: Women in Major American Fiction of the Sixties* (Urbana: University of Illinois Press, 1976), p. 96.

2. Leslie A. Fiedler, *Waiting for the End* (New York: Stein and Day, 1964), pp. 64–65.

Bibliography

I. WORKS BY PHILIP ROTH

Books

Goodbye, Columbus. Boston: Houghton Mifflin Co., 1959.
Letting Go. New York: Random House, 1962.
When She Was Good. New York: Random House, 1967.
Portnoy's Complaint. New York: Random House, 1969.
Our Gang. New York: Random House, 1971.
The Breast. New York: Holt, Rinehart and Winston, 1972.
The Great American Novel. New York: Holt, Rinehart and Winston, 1973.
My Life as a Man. New York: Holt, Rinehart and Winston, 1974.
Reading Myself and Others. New York: Farrar, Straus and Giroux, 1975.
The Professor of Desire. New York: Farrar, Straus and Giroux, 1977.
The Ghost Writer. New York: Farrar, Straus and Giroux, 1979.
A Philip Roth Reader. New York: Farrar, Straus and Giroux, 1980.

Uncollected Short Stories

"The Day It Snowed," *Chicago Review*, 8 (Fall 1954), 34–45.
"The Contest for Aaron Gold," *Epoch*, 5–6 (Fall 1955), 37–51.
"Heard Melodies Are Sweeter," *Esquire*, August 1958, p. 58.
"Expect the Vandals," *Esquire*, December 1958, pp. 208–28.

"The Love Vessel," *Dial 1*, 1 (Fall 1959), 41–68.

"Good Girl," *Cosmopolitan,* May 1960, pp. 98–103.

"The Mistaken," *American Judaism,* 10 (Fall 1960), 10.

"Novotny's Pain," *The New Yorker,* October 27, 1962, pp. 46–56.

"Psychoanalytic Special," *Esquire,* November 1963, p. 106.

"On the Air," *New American Review,* 10 (August 1970), 7–49.

II.   WORKS ABOUT PHILIP ROTH

Allen, Mary. "Philip Roth: When She Was Good She Was Horrid," *The Necessary Blankness: Women in Major American Fiction of the Sixties.* Urbana: University of Illinois Press, 1976, pp. 70–96.

Alter, Robert. "The Education of David Kepesh," *Partisan Review,* 46 (1979), 478–81.

Atlas, James. "A Visit with Philip Roth," *New York Times Book Review,* September 2, 1979, p. 1.

Bettelheim, Bruno. "Portnoy Psychoanalyzed," *Midstream,* 15 (June–July 1969), 3–10.

Deer, Irving and Harriet. "Philip Roth and the Crisis in American Fiction," *Minnesota Review,* 6 (No. 4, 1966), 353–60.

Detweiler, Robert. "Philip Roth and the Test of the Dialogic Life," *Four Spiritual Crises in Mid-Century American Fiction.* Gainesville: University of Florida Monographs, No. 14, 1963, pp. 25–35.

Edwards, Thomas R. *New York Times Book Review,* May 6, 1973, p. 27.

Fiedler, Leslie A. *Waiting for the End.* New York: Stein and Day, 1964.

Gass, William. "The Sporting News," *New York Review of Books,* May 31, 1973, p. 7.

Hicks, Granville. "Literary Horizons," *Saturday Review,* February 22, 1969, pp. 38–39.

Howe, Irving. "The Suburbs of Babylon," *New Republic,* June 15, 1959, p. 17.

————. "Philip Roth Reconsidered," *Commentary*, 54 (December 1972), 69–77.

Lehmann-Haupt, Christopher. "Philip Roth's Bathtub Novel," *New York Times*, May 14, 1973, p. 29.

Leonard, John. "Fathers and Ghosts," *New York Review of Books*, October 25, 1979, p. 4.

Maddocks, Melvin. "Make It New," *Time*, June 10, 1974, p. 92.

Mannes, Marya. "A Dissent from Marya Mannes," *Saturday Review*, February 22, 1969, p. 39.

McDaniel, John N. *The Fiction of Philip Roth*. Haddonfield, N.J.: Haddonfield House, 1974.

Meeter, Glenn. *Philip Roth and Bernard Malamud: A Critical Essay*. Grand Rapids, Michigan: William B. Eerdmans, 1968.

Pinsker, Sanford. *The Comedy That "Hoits": An Essay on the Fiction of Philip Roth*. Columbia: University of Missouri Press, 1975.

Prescott, Peter S. "Roth in Full Flower," *Newsweek*, September 10, 1979, pp. 72–73.

Raban, Jonathan. "The New Philip Roth," *Novel*, 2 (Winter 1969), 153–63.

Rodgers, Bernard F., Jr. *Philip Roth: A Bibliography*. Scarecrow Author Bibliographies, No. 19. Metuchen, N.J.: Scarecrow Press, 1974.

————. *Philip Roth*. Boston: Twayne Publishers, 1978.

Rosenthal, Raymond. "Weak Men, Furious Women," *New Leader*, 50 (June 19, 1967), 19.

Sabiston, Elizabeth. "A New Fable for Critics: Philip Roth's *The Breast*," *International Fiction Review*, 2 (1975), 27–34.

Schott, Webster. "No Joy in Mudville," *Washington Post Book World*, May 13, 1973, p. 7.

Shechner, Mark. "Philip Roth," *Partisan Review*, Fall 1974, pp. 410–27.

Sheppard, R. Z. "The Novel: Very Warm for May," *Time*, 101 (May 7, 1973), 65.

Siegel, Ben. "The Myths of Summer: Philip Roth's *The Great American Novel*", *Contemporary Literature*, 17 (Spring 1976), 171–90.

Solotaroff, Theodore. "Philip Roth and the Jewish Moral-
    ists," *Chicago Review*, 13 (Winter 1959), 87–99.
————. "The Journey of Philip Roth," *Atlantic*, 223
    (April 1969), 64–72.
————. "Fiction," *Esquire*, October 1972, pp. 82–84.
Tanner, Tony. "Fictionalized Recall—or 'The Settling of
    Scores! The Pursuit of Dreams!'" *City of Words:
    American Fiction 1950–1970*. New York: Harper and
    Row, 1971, pp. 295–321.
Towers, Robert. "The Lesson of the Master," *New York
    Times Book Review*, September 2, 1979, p. 1.
Trachtenberg, Stanley. "The Hero in Stasis," *Critique*, 7
    (Winter 1964/65), 5–17.
Wisse, Ruth. "Requiem in Several Voices," *The Schlemiel
    as Modern Hero*. Chicago: University of Chicago
    Press, 1971, pp. 118–23.
Wolff, Geoffrey. "Beyond Portnoy," *Newsweek*, August 3,
    1970, pp. 66–77.

Index

MODERN LITERATURE SERIES

In the same series (continued from page ii)

DATE DUE			